ROCK CLIMBING ANCHORS:
A Comprehensive Guide

THE MOUNTAINEERS BOOKS

ROCK CLIMBING ANCHORS:
A Comprehensive Guide

Craig Luebben

MOUNTAINEERS
OUTDOOR EXPERT
series

THE MOUNTAINEERS BOOKS
*is the nonprofit publishing arm of The Mountaineers Club,
an organization founded in 1906 and dedicated to the exploration,
preservation, and enjoyment of outdoor and wilderness areas.*

1001 SW Klickitat Way, Suite 201, Seattle, WA 98134

First edition, 2007

Manufactured in the United States of America

Acquiring Editor: Christine Hosler
Project Editor: Mary Metz
Developmental Editor: Christine Clifton-Thornton
Copy Editor: Colin Chisholm
Cover and Book Design: The Mountaineers Books
Layout: Mayumi Thompson
Illustrator: Jeremy Collins
Photographer: All photographs by the author unless otherwise noted.
Cover photograph: *Karissa Dunbar prepares to clip on Angular Motion (5.12a), Carver, Oregon.*
© Brian Stevenson/Aurora Photos
Back cover photograph: *Guides Bill Libertore, Matt Wade, and Joe Crocker rappelling off Frigidaire Buttress, Red Rocks Nevada*
Frontispiece: *Topher Donahue spicing it up on* Lock of Rages (5.12R), *Rocky Mountain National Park, Colorado.*

Library of Congress Cataloging-in-Publication Data
Luebben, Craig.
  Rock climbing anchors : a comprehensive guide / by Craig Luebben. — 1st ed.
     p. cm.
  Includes index.
  ISBN-13: 978-1-59485-006-6
  ISBN-10: 1-59485-006-2
  1. Rock climbing—Equipment and supplies. 2. Rock climbing—Safety measures. I. Title.
  GV200.15.L84 2006
  796.522'3—dc22
                              2006024760

 Printed on recycled paper

Contents

CHAPTER 1
Anchor Basics

Dedication

This book is dedicated to all outdoor educators. By helping others discover, explore, and enjoy the outdoors, you enrich countless lives. Mark and Marcia Van Skiver helped me and some friends begin skiing and backpacking at age fourteen, and high school math teacher Barb Evert took us skiing and climbing

Colorado's fourteeners. These early adventures had a profound influence on my life. Learning never stops in the outdoors. Last season my great ski teachers Chad Vander Ham and Doug Coombs showed me how to get down when it's really steep. May you rest in peace, brothers.

Acknowledgments

One day in 1984 Chuck Grossman and Kent Wheeler thought they were on the *Petit Grepon* in Rocky Mountain National Park when they were really on *The Saber*, a harder and more serious climb. That's where I met them, as we all raced to beat an electrical storm. The following week I had to submit ten ideas for a wide crack protection device to my mechanical engineering professor Jaime Cardenas-Garcia. On the hike down from *The Saber* Chuck mentioned the words "expandable tube": that became the eleventh idea, and ultimately the Big Bro expandable tube chock.

Through marketing the Big Bro I met the *Rock & Ice* editors and began writing for them. This led to working on some John Long books as the technical editor, including his first *Climbing Anchors* book. The next evolution was working for *Climbing* magazine, and writing several instructional books of my own. Without Chuck there would have been no Big Bro, and probably no magazine articles or books, including this one. Thanks, Chuck.

I'm also grateful to my project editors at The Mountaineers Books whose patience I have taxed time and again (hey, it's not easy to write and photograph one of these books!). Christine Hosler directed this project from beginning to end, providing guidance and pressure without cracking the whip too hard while Mary Metz oversaw the project and steered the book through its final stages. Developmental editor Christine Clifton-Thornton taught me how to actually write a book, and she helped immensely with the organization. Copy editor and climber Colin Chisholm took the book through its home stretch, making sure that the photos and captions jived (they often did not), and making the book readable. Mayumi Thompson masterfully designed the layout.

Some of my friends gave the text a look-over and made valuable suggestions.

Thanks to Colorado Mountain Club mountaineering instructor Meredith Lazaroff for reviewing an early version of the book, and to Casey Bernal and Silvia Luebben for busting me when my climbing physics was wrong.

All climbers owe thanks to Jim Ewing, research and development director of Sterling Rope company, for his tireless testing of ropes and anchoring systems, including his recent tests showing that cordelettes sometimes do not equalize as well as we hoped. Thanks to John Long for helping me get started in this business, and for his research into anchoring systems. And thanks to all the participants in the online *rockclimbing.com* thread pertaining to anchors, equalizing, and the cordelette versus sliding X versus equalizer. Many new anchor rigging designs were created in this thread, and some of the ideas are used in the Belay Anchors chapter.

I also owe thanks to Malcolm Daly of Trango for hiring me as a climbing guide at Colorado State University in 1981, for marketing the Big Bro, and for the million other things that he has done for the climbing community. Thanks also to my fellow American Mountain Guides Association (AMGA) rock guide instructors and students who have given me many ideas, especially Jeff and Steve Banks who showed me some new sling anchoring techniques.

The gear shown in this book is the best stuff currently available; it's the gear that my climbing partners and I use regularly. Much appreciation goes to Metolius, Misty Mountain, Omega Pacific, Petzl, Sterling Rope, Trango, and Wild Country for providing gear for the photographs.

Individually I'd like to thank Caroline Brodsky, Malcolm Daly, Jim Ewing, Lisa Gnade, Mike Grimm, Goose Kearse, Michael Lane, Seth Murray, Paul Nyland, Steve Petro, Doug Phillips, Rudy Rasmussen, and Brooke Sandahl. I also owe appreciation to Gary Neptune for allowing me to photograph some historical chocks in his climbing equipment museum at Neptune Mountaineering in Boulder, Colorado.

Thank you to the models that grace these pages. They include some of America's best climbers, including two climbing World Cup Champions. Thanks to Mike Auldridge, Mia Axon, Francisco Blanco, Cassie Bloss, Katie Brown, Tommy Caldwell, Stacy Carrera, Joe Crocker, Cameron Cross, Steph Davis, Topher Donahue, Sarah Gross, Skip Harper, Kennan Harvey, Lynn Hill, Andy Johnson, Brad Jackson, Sue Kligerman, David Lazaroff, Bill Libertore, Curtis Love, Giulia Luebben, Silvia Luebben, Charlie Mace, Anna McConica, Carol McConica, Jeremy Medley, Pascal Perrier, Kathy Plate, Jeff Skoloda, Laura Strauss, Kevin Stricker, Lauri Stricker, Toti Valdez, and Matt Wade.

Introduction

Gravity: The tireless force that pulls two bodies together. The more massive the bodies and the closer they are, the stronger the pull. Earth's huge mass creates an enormous gravitational force that traps the atmosphere, holds the planet together, drives glaciers and rivers, and makes climbing what it is—fun and challenging, yet sometimes frightening, perilous, and hard. Gravity lurks and lingers, always ready to pluck a climber from his tenuous stance. When a climber does fall it's up to the rope and anchors to catch him.

Climbing anchors allow us to "safely" defy gravity. We use them to build belay and rappel stations, set top ropes, and protect a lead climber. Solid anchors and proper rope techniques can prevent a fall from turning into a catastrophe; bad anchors are an accident waiting to happen.

Setting anchors is simple and straightforward on many climbs; on other routes, finding the anchors and engineering the protection system can be a significant part of the climb's challenge. For some climbers the problem-solving of creating anchors is one of the many appeals of rock climbing. For others setting anchors is just a duty to keep the climbing safe. Either way, having a large repertoire of anchoring techniques makes climbing safer and more efficient.

The information in *Rock Climbing Anchors: A Comprehensive Guide* is based upon nearly three decades of climbing, 25 years of guiding, and my study of mechanical engineering. It's a mix of theory and practical application.

Over the years I've had the great fortune to climb with many of America's best climbers, and I've worked with instructors from the AMGA, teaching bright young climbers how to be good, safe rock climbing guides. Besides having a ton of fun, I've learned many skills and tricks from my wide net of talented climbing partners.

Writing this book began in 1984, when

I was required to produce a 110-page thesis on the Big Bro tube chock design to earn my mechanical engineering degree at Colorado State University. The document included extensive sections on anchoring systems, rope dynamics, and climbing physics. Since then I've conducted several strength tests of cams, cordelettes, and ice screws, both in the field and in the testing lab at Sterling Rope Company. I've also tested and reviewed camming devices, ropes, and other climbing equipment for *Climbing* and *Rock & Ice* magazines several times.

Some of the ideas and techniques presented here come from the guide's perspective; these are systems that are used day-in and day-out by thousands of guides around the world. Other information comes from the light-and-fast school, where speed, efficiency, and skill trump the urge to build big complex belay anchors.

Many valid climbing styles, rope systems, and anchor rigging techniques exist—there are dozens of ways to crack an egg. This is where creativity meets science. There are lots of options for building an anchor; in the end it needs to be strong enough for the given situation and convenient to use. The key is to understand the potential forces. Being able to do it fast, clean, and without excessive gear increases the climbing team's potential for tackling longer routes.

On two opposite extremes, a team of intermediate climbers may set as many anchors in a four-pitch route as a speed team does in twenty pitches. This variation among climbing teams is fine, because everyone is (hopefully) having fun and accomplishing their objectives. While the intermediates might think the speed climbers are irresponsible or crazy, the speed climbers are substituting climbing skill, advanced rope techniques, and risk tolerance for heavy reliance on gear to achieve their goal of climbing *fast*.

Most instructional books can be accused of encouraging protocol-based solutions to problems. But the climbing landscape is too complex and the variables too many to be served well by protocol. A climber needs the flexibility to craft a solution for each situation. Protocol is necessary for beginners and somewhat for intermediates. For anyone seeking to become a good climber, though, the goal is to become educated and experienced so you can consistently and quickly make good, judgment-based decisions. I hope this book will help you on that quest.

HOW TO USE THIS BOOK

The material presented here is geared toward intermediate to advanced rock climbers, alpinists, and mountaineers. We assume the reader has basic climbing skills and knowledge, including: belaying, communication signals, moving over rock, rappelling, top-roping, and lead climbing. Climbers lacking familiarity with these techniques may find *Rock Climbing: Mastering Basic Skills*, by this author, a better starting point.

Chapter 1 focuses on anchors for top-roping, rappelling, sport climbing, leading trad routes, and belay stations. It discusses the forces generated in a fall, how many pieces to set for an anchor, how V-angles can increase forces, how to build and equalize multidirectional anchors, how to attach yourself to anchors, belay techniques, and how to evaluate rock quality.

Chapter 2 covers natural anchors such as trees, boulders, blocks, flakes, chockstones, horns and threads, and fixed anchors such as pitons and bolts. Chapter 3 discusses all types of chocks including wired nuts, hex nuts, Tri-cams, sliding nuts, and Big Bros. Chapter 4 examines cams, including how they evolved, how they work, how to place or remove them, and how to discern between good and bad placements.

The first four chapters provide the foundation for the anchor systems shown later in the book. Chapters 5–9 can stand alone—pick and choose the chapters that pique your climbing interests.

Chapter 5 discusses top-rope and rappel anchors, and chapter 6 talks about protecting sport climbs. Chapter 7 covers how to rig trad belay anchors using a cordelette, slings, or a climbing rope. Chapter 8 explains considerations for protecting the lead on traditional routes. The final chapter explains how physics affects the forces in lead climbing falls, what types of falls are the most risky, and how to reduce the impact in high force falls.

Appendix 1 discusses cords, webbing, and carabiners. A second appendix shows a variety of knots used for rigging anchor systems, while the third appendix includes equations for those who didn't get enough physics in chapter 9.

FURTHER TRAINING

Each climber in a team shares responsibility for keeping the team safe and self-reliant, and each must be knowledgeable about climbing anchors and rope work. If you're always relying on your partners to take care of you, what are you going to do if they get hurt and need you to get the team up or down? Get professional instruction if you're a beginner or if you have glaring holes in your climbing knowledge.

Safe climbing requires good anchoring skills. This text covers many techniques, but it is still only a collection of words, photographs, and illustrations. Climbers seeking to develop their anchoring skills should take an intensive, on-the-rocks anchor clinic with an American Mountain Guides Association (AMGA) certified rock guide, or a guide who works for an AMGA-accredited school. Material found on these pages will supplement and reinforce such a course. Experienced climbers can use the book to reinforce old ideas and to learn some new ones.

Climbing gear and techniques are constantly evolving. Climbers of all experience levels should stay current by reading magazine technique articles and updated instructional manuals. Keep your eye out for product recalls, which happen all too frequently in the climbing industry.

ENVIRONMENTAL CONSIDERATIONS

Climbing has become so popular that many areas are being overrun. As climbers we have a duty to help preserve our climbing areas, to keep them beautiful and open to climbing. This means using trails and avoiding side paths and shortcuts; avoiding needless killing of plants or trees; picking up trash (including tape scraps and cigarette butts), whether it is yours or not; minimizing the use of chalk tick marks, and cleaning them when you're done; burying or carrying human waste (or better, settling these needs *before* going to the crag); avoiding making excessive noise; and keeping pets from chasing wildlife or annoying other climbers.

CLIMBING ORGANIZATIONS

The Access Fund is a climbing advocacy group that promotes conservation and climbing access. Anyone who loves climbing should join the Access Fund to help their mission of keeping climbing areas open and promoting healthy stewardship of the land. *www.accessfund.com*; (303) 545-6772. **Leave No Trace** promotes low impact use of the outdoors, and teaches responsible outdoor practices through their training programs. *www.lnt.org*; (303) 442-8222.

The International Mountaineering and Climbing Federation (UIAA, Union Internationale Des Associations D'Alpinisme) is a federation of 97 national climbing and mountaineering associations from 68 countries. UIAA supports all forms of climbing and mountaineering, encourages environmentally acceptable climbing practices, governs international climbing competitions, promotes cooperation and interaction among climbers from all nations, and seeks to minimize the hazards involved in climbing. To this end the UIAA safety commission has created testing standards for climbing equipment to ensure that available gear is suitable for climbing. Gear must pass a battery of tests in a UIAA-approved testing laboratory to receive UIAA certification. When buying equipment look for the UIAA safety label to ensure that it passes UIAA standards.

The European Union has also created standards for climbing gear based on the old UIAA standards. Gear passing this standard will be marked with an EN or CEN label. The current UIAA standards may have stricter requirements than the EN standards. For more information go to *www.uiaa.ch*.

AMERICAN MOUNTAIN GUIDES ASSOCIATION

The American Mountain Guides Association (AMGA) is a non-profit organization that trains and certifies guides in three disciplines—rock climbing, alpine climbing, and ski mountaineering. To become *certified* an individual guide must take courses, work with mentors, gain extensive climbing and guiding experience, and pass rigorous multiday field examinations.

A guide service or school can be *accredited* by AMGA after a review of their safety, training, and administrative practices. I recommend hiring AMGA-certified climbing guides, or guides working for accredited services. Otherwise you may be wasting your money, your time, or worse. To find a list of certified guides, contact AMGA at (303) 271-0984, *www .amga.com.*

WARNING!
READ THE FOLLOWING BEFORE USING THIS BOOK

Climbing is dangerous. You can be killed or seriously injured while rock climbing. No book can describe or predict all the hazardous and complex situations that can occur while climbing, and the techniques described here are not appropriate for all climbing situations.

The information provided here is intended to supplement formal, competent instruction. Do not rely on this text as your primary source of rock climbing information—a simple misinterpretation could be disastrous. Climbing safely requires good judgment based on experience, competent instruction, and a realistic understanding of your personal skills and limitations. Even if you do everything right you can still get injured or killed.

This book contains only the personal opinions of the author and it focuses exclusively on climbing anchors so it lacks coverage of a great deal of important climbing safety technique and procedures. The author and publisher make no warranties, expressed or implied, that the information contained here is accurate or reliable. Further, the author and publisher make no warranties as to fitness for a particular purpose or that this book is merchantable, and they assume no liability for readers who participate in any activities discussed here. Use of this text implies that you accept responsibility for your own climbing safety, and you assume the risk of injury or death.

CHAPTER 1

Tommy Caldwell and Mike Auldridge climbing the ultraclassic Naked Edge

Anchor Basics

One of the beauties of rock climbing is its amazing diversity. Sea cliffs, high alpine faces, desert towers, water-carved canyons, random crags in the woods: the geographical possibilities are endless. Add in the different rock types: impeccable granite, wildly featured limestone, flaw-less sandstone, and myriad other igneous, metamorphic, and sedimentary rocks, ranging from choss to totally solid. You can also change the angle, from tip-toe friction slabs, to striking vertical faces, to gymnastic roofs and caves; or pick a crack of any size, from finger tips to chimneys. You can pursue boulder problems, eighty-foot sport routes, multipitch gear routes, or massive walls.

Then you have the protection factor, ranging from no-commitment top ropes to athletic clip-ups, and from splitter cracks that devour pro to dicey, runout, rarely climbed test pieces. And how much effort do you want to spend? You can choose from easy romps, full-throttle onsights, and multiday redpoint projects. Given all this variety, one thing remains common: most rock climbing (besides bouldering and free soloing) relies on anchors for creating the safety system.

In this chapter we'll discuss how anchors are used for:

- top-roping
- rappelling
- sport climbing
- leading traditional routes
- multipitch belay stations

Then we'll discuss:

- what kind of forces can be generated in a fall
- how many pieces to set in an anchor
- how to build equalized, redundant anchors
- avoiding large V-angles that amplify forces
- creating multidirectional anchors

- attaching yourself to the anchor with the rope, slings, or a daisy chain
- pre-equalizing versus self-equalizing
- using the appropriate belay technique
- evaluating rock quality

TOP-ROPE ANCHORS

When top-roping, the rope usually runs from the climber, up to anchors at the top of the route, then back down to the belayer. This setup is called a "slingshot" top rope. With the rope anchored above the climber the belayer can immediately halt a fall, which makes top-roping one of the safest ways to climb. Depending on the situation, anchors can be set at the lip of the cliff, or back from the edge and extended with slings or cord over the cliff edge.

In some cases the climbing team may anchor the belayer atop the cliff. This setup works well if the base of the cliff is difficult to access. Chapter 5 shows how to rig the system whether the belayer is above or below the climb.

RAPPEL ANCHORS

If no reasonable walk-off exists on an established climb you'll find fixed rappel anchors for descending. Fixed rap anchors run the gamut from completely solid to totally sketchy—it's up to you to decide which before trusting your life to the anchors. Chapter 5 covers how to evaluate fixed rappel anchors, how to back them up, and how to rig rappel stations (to clean up messy stations or create new ones). It also explains much of the standard hardware found on the cliffs.

Jeff Skoloda top-roping at Rotary Park, Horsetooth Reservoir, Colorado

Cameron Cross rappelling off 1%, Vinales, Cuba

SPORT CLIMBING ANCHORS

Climbers protect sport routes by clipping pre-placed anchor bolts. Chapter 6 discusses how to evaluate existing bolts, how to rig bolted belay anchors, and how to back up the bolts at a belay station.

Sarah Gross belaying the leader in Red River Gorge, Kentucky

Pascale Perrier clipping bolts on Flyin' Hyena *(5.12), Vinales, Cuba*

BELAY ANCHORS

On a multipitch route the lead climber sets belay anchors at the end of each pitch and belays her partner up. When the partner arrives at the belay station they reorganize the rack and one of them leads above. When the leader starts up the next pitch, the belay anchors provide the climbing team's sole security (save the climber's skill), with a high-force fall possible.

A good belay anchor generally has multiple anchors rigged together with cord or webbing to create a master point for clipping in. Chapter 7 shows how to rig belay anchors that are convenient, quick, clean—and bombproof. It also shows how to deal with some tricky anchoring situations, and how to make do with minimal amounts of gear.

LEAD PROTECTION

Traditional, or "trad," climbers set their own protection anchors while leading to protect against a fall. The first climber leads a pitch, placing protection as she climbs.

If she falls, she'll fall twice the distance to her last protection—providing that it holds. After she finishes the pitch and anchors herself, she belays the second climber, who removes the gear as he climbs. He has a top rope, so climbing second is safer and less psychologically demanding than leading. The second climber often leads the next pitch. Chapter 8 provides information on protecting a pitch when lead climbing.

Kathy Plate setting a cam on the overhanging Ruffis (5.11), Vedauwoo, Wyoming

Hallucinogen Wall (VI A3+), Black Canyon of the Gunnison, Colorado. Steph Davis leading, Kennan Harvey belaying, and the author fretting over the ancient belay bolts

AID AND BIG WALL CLIMBING

Wall climbers are probably the most in-tune with the subtleties of anchoring—they often spend hours aid climbing a single pitch, setting anchors barely strong enough to hold body weight. At the end of the pitch they set a belay anchor that must withstand hauling, jugging, and the possibility of catching a gear-laden climber. This book does not cover specialized aid gear or techniques but it does provide information that is useful for aid climbing.

CLEAN CLIMBING

When I began climbing in 1978, I learned much of my limited knowledge from Royal Robbins's *Beginning Rockcraft* and *Advanced Rockcraft* books. When those books were created, some of the primary anchors used by climbers were pitons, which were beaten in and out of cracks with a hammer. The problem was, all of that pounding destroyed the rock. When chocks, and later cams, became available, most climbers embraced the new "clean climbing" ethic, using the new gear that could be placed and removed by hand, without scarring the rock. But I didn't know that at the time.

On my very first climb I was leading and pounding pitons, until some climbers yelled up, "Hey! We don't use those pitons anymore!" After that I embraced clean climbing too. Pitons are still useful for some alpine and aid climbs.

When a climber places a bolt it becomes a permanent fixture in the rock. Bolts have enabled the creation of hundreds of thousands of great climbs (and more than a few trashy ones) around the world, but they definitely change the character of a cliff and an area. It is up to each climber to use good judgment and follow local tradition when placing pitons or bolts, and to embrace clean climbing—by using removable anchors that do not require a hammer or drill—when the rock allows.

FORCES ON CLIMBING ANCHORS

When considering the possible forces on anchors, it's essential to discern between *body weight* situations and *leader fall forces*.

Body Weight. When top-roping, the climber is below the anchor; the maximum load on the anchors will be the climber's weight and part of the belayer's weight; if the climber falls with slack in the rope, the force can be somewhat higher, but still well below the strength of solid anchors. If the rock is less than vertical, the force on the anchors decreases with the angle of the rock.

When rappelling, if the descent is smooth, the anchors hold only the climber's weight. A jerky rappel can drastically increase the force on the anchors, but solid rappel anchors will still easily withstand such a load.

The construction and rescue industries use "safety factors" for calculating the load that a structure must be capable of withstanding. For some applications they use a safety factor of five—any structure or system must be five times stronger than any foreseeable load. Three solid anchors pre-equalized with a cordelette might hold more than 40 kN (9000 pounds), giving an impressive safety factor of 10 to 20: the anchor is ten to twenty times stronger than needed for the body weight loads created during top-roping or rappelling.

Leader Fall Forces. When lead climbing you can often toss the safety factor out the window. Lead falls usually come onto a single piece of protection, and the pulley effect (explained later in this chapter) can increase the impact force on the protection by

FALL FORCES

Body weight forces created during top-roping and rappelling are low compared to the huge forces possible in a leader fall.

60 to 70 percent above the force on the falling climber. In the worst cases—when the climber is close to the belay and little rope is out—falls can come close to or exceed the strength of some climbing protection, especially tiny nuts, small cams, carabiners with the gates pushed open, sketchy fixed gear, or anchors set in poor rock. Only bomber pieces can hold these worst-case falls.

The force in a vertical or overhanging leader fall is determined by the weight of the climber, the length of the fall, and by how fast the fall is stopped. The saving grace to high leader fall forces is the dynamic rope, which stretches to dampen the climber's deceleration. In hard leader falls, the dynamic belay—in which some rope slips through the belay device, or possibly the belayer's body gets lifted—can also slow the falling climber's rate of deceleration and reduce the peak impact force. The rope slippage is not generally intentional though sometimes it is; it is caused when the rope pulling force on the brake hand exceeds the climber's grip strength (belay gloves are nice here). Autolocking belay devices like the Petzl GriGri or Trango Cinch limit rope slippage and stop the fall *fast;* this increases the impact force but decreases the falling distance.

A load-limiting runner—one with stitches that blow out as the runner gets loaded—also slows the falling climber's deceleration rate and reduces the peak force. Once all the energy-absorbing stitches are blown you have a full-strength runner that will allow the force to increase if the fall has not completely stopped. Ice climbers love load-limiters because ice pro is often sketchy. Load limiters make the most difference on falls near the belay where peak forces are high.

The force in a leader fall is roughly proportional to the climber's weight. Lighter climbers have a better chance that mediocre gear will catch a fall. Since the UIAA uses 80 kg (176 lbs) test weights in its rope certification tests, climbers heavier than this might take extra precautions, like setting more protection, equalizing mediocre pieces, using load-limiters on mediocre protection near the belay, and climbing on thicker ropes.

A leader needs to know when the forces may be high and place solid protection, back off, or climb with perfect control. Chapter 9 discusses climbing physics, forces on lead protection, and fall factors.

High force situations:

- falling close to belay (high fall factor)
- long falling distance (high fall factor)
- autolocking belay device (static belay)
- heavy leader (high momentum)

UNITS OF MEASURE

Most countries in the world have adopted the metric system, which uses Newtons (N) and meters (m) to measure force and distance. In the United States we are stuck using pounds and feet from the British system, even though the Brits had the good sense to abandon it. The unit of force used to rate climbing gear is the kiloNewton (kN), which equals 1000 Newtons or 225 pounds. In this book we use metric units with English units shown in parentheses.

HOW MANY ANCHORS?

When setting anchors for rappelling, top-roping, or building a belay station, two *good* bolts or three *bomber* pieces are usually adequate. When belaying a leader, an extra anchor is sometimes added to hold an upward pull.

Bomber means BOMBER—able to stop a truck or halt a train. If the pieces are not BOMBER, add more and equalize them. Likewise, if the pieces are small nuts and cams (and by definition, not bomber), or if the rock quality is alarming, add more anchors. Having bomber anchors serves two purposes: it keeps you from hitting the deck *and* allows you to relax and enjoy climbing. Sometimes I'll set an extra piece just for peace of mind (especially in a hanging belay).

As in so many areas of life, quality over quantity is the mantra. Two bomber belay anchors are more reassuring than six shifty micronuts and microcams. On a multipitch climb the first piece of lead protection on each pitch protects the belay anchors from a severe impact, and it makes a fall easier for the belayer to catch. The first piece is so critical that it can be considered part of the belay anchor. If the first protection isn't good, find better pro as soon as possible.

In alpine situations the climbing team sometimes relies on one or two pieces for an anchor. For safety the belayer should

ERNEST

The problem with acronyms is that they encourage protocol rather than judgment-based decision making. The climber thinks, "If my anchor is ERNEST I am set," rather than analyzing the situation and crafting an appropriate, efficient solution. Still, acronyms are a useful mnemonic device for learning, and they can help you remember some key points.

When rigging multipoint anchors for a belay station, rappel station, or top-rope, the acronym ERNEST sums up many important considerations:

E = Equalized. The load is distributed somewhat equally among the individual anchors, so the final rigged anchor achieves maximum strength.

R= Redundant. All components of the anchor are backed up, so any single failure does not result in a catastrophe.

NE= No Extension. If any anchor fails, extension in the rigging material is minimized to protect the remaining anchor(s) from receiving a higher impact load.

S= Solid. Each component and the overall system must be solid enough for the situation.

T=Timely. Building the anchors is fast and efficient.

belay off his harness and bolster the anchors with his stance. If the climber falls, the belayer takes the weight on his braced body, with the anchors as a backup. This might be fine for belaying a second climber, but if the leader falls onto such a belay the result can be disastrous. The body belay strategy has little place in high-angle rock climbing, where good anchors are usually available and falling forces can be huge.

Occasionally a belay, or more often a rappel, will be anchored off a single, living, well-rooted, large tree. Trusting a single tree is a judgment call that must be made by the climbing team, but obviously a large diameter, healthy, well-rooted tree is more than strong enough to serve as the sole climbing anchor.

HOW IMPORTANT IS EQUALIZATION?

By definition equalization means distributing the load evenly among two or more pieces to increase the strength of the overall anchor. It's like putting all your team members on the rope in a tug-of-war. If you let two of them sit, ready to work only when disaster is imminent, you'll never achieve the team's maximum pulling strength. Likewise in an anchor: if all of the pieces are not sharing the load, it's not as strong as it can be.

Often you don't need all of the tug-of-war team members pulling, though. When top-roping or rappelling, it's like having grade-school kids pulling against NFL linemen. Two-thirds of the linemen can sit down and you still have no contest. The same with the anchors: if you have three bomber cams, each capable of holding 14kN (3150 pounds), any of the pieces can easily hold the 2–4 kN (450–900 pounds) maximum force, with the rest serving as a backup, so equalization isn't so crucial.

When the leader is climbing directly above the belay with no protection, your anchors are up against the NFL linemen. You want them all working to produce maximum strength, so it's smart to equalize. The same with mediocre or bad belay anchors or lead protection—setting more pieces and equalizing them makes them stronger.

For maximum strength you would actually want to spread the load proportionately to the strength of each individual piece—stronger pieces would hold more force and weaker pieces would hold less. But no one could predict the exact strength of each piece, or rig to distribute precise fractions of the load to each piece. Instead, when it's important to equalize we strive for equal load distribution among the pieces: ideally a two-piece anchor gets a fifty-fifty split, three pieces hold one-third each, and a four-piece anchor spreads 25 percent of the load to each piece.

Some rigging systems equalize better than others. So it comes back to judgment-based decision making: you have to determine what kind of force might hit the anchor, how strong the individual pieces are, and what type of anchor rigging is most convenient and strong enough for the job. In climbing it often pays to be conservative; if in doubt, equalize.

PRE-EQUALIZED ANCHORS

Pre-equalized rigging creates a convenient "work station" at the anchor, and it's a fast, simple way to build anchors that are redundant and allow no extension if an anchor blows. A pre-equalized anchor consists of a cordelette or double-length sling extend-ing to each piece and tied-off to create a master point that connects the climbers to all of the anchors. The single clipping point is especially convenient when one climber leads many pitches in a row, or when the team has more than two climbers.

The downside to pre-equalizing? It doesn't always distribute the load equally between the pieces. If the anchors are spread horizontally, with the leg lengths roughly equal and adjusted well for the direction of pull, a pre-equalized sling or cordelette *can* spread the load fairly well. In one series of tests that I conducted at the Sterling Rope

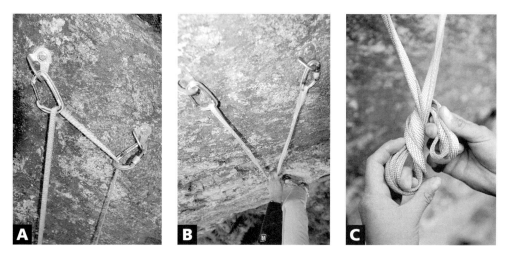

Pre-equalizing a double-length sling (one that fits nicely over-the-shoulder when doubled) is one of the simplest ways to create a redundant, somewhat equalized two-point anchor.
A. *Clip the sling into both bolts.*
B. *Pull two loops down between the bolts, toward the anticipated direction of loading. Keep the sling's stitching (or knot) up close to one of the bolts.*
C. *Tie a figure eight or overhand knot in the sling to create a master point, while keeping the sling oriented toward the anticipated direction of pull. If enough sling is not available for a figure eight, an overhand knot will work fine, but a figure eight is easier to untie after being loaded.*

testing lab, three-point anchors that were spread horizontally and rigged with a cordelette consistently held above 40 kN (9000 pounds).

If the loading direction varies though, all of the force can go onto one piece. A single piece can also take the brunt of the force if it's connected to a short leg in the cordelette because that leg will stretch the least. If the anchors are spread vertically the leg lengths will be unequal, and so will the load distribution.

With bomber pieces it's hard to create a load that makes them fail no matter how you rig them. Even if all the stars align against you to create a worst-case fall onto the belay anchors, by the time that a solid piece did fail, most of the fall's momentum would be gone and the other good anchors would easily handle the remaining load.

If the pieces aren't bomber you can create enough force in a fall to rip them out. In this case, or if the loading direction on the anchors might change, rigging with the sliding X or the equalizer (see next section) will distribute the load better and give more strength than a pre-equalized setup.

Many guides tie their cordelette into a loop with a flat overhand knot because it's

D. Tie into a locking carabiner clipped to the master point (sometimes called the "power point") and lock it to connect into both anchors.

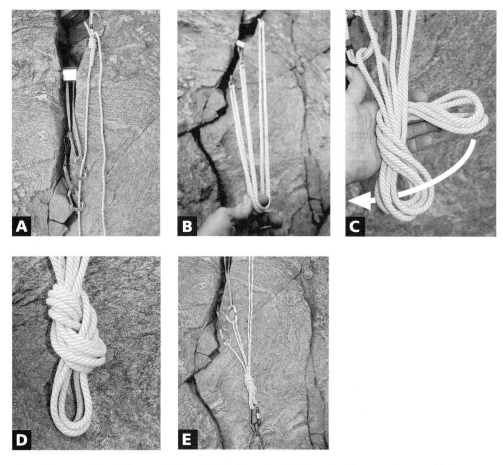

A cordelette—a 5- to 6.5- meter (16- to 22-foot) length of 5.5- or 6-millimeter diameter high-strength cord, or 7-millimeter diameter perlon—conveniently rigs three- or four-point anchors to ERNEST standards. To rig the cordelette:

A. Tie the cordelette into a loop with a double fisherman's or other suitable knot, and clip the cordelette to all the anchors.

B. Pull down a length of cord between each anchor, in the expected direction of loading.

C. Tie a figure eight knot in the cordelette, or an overhand if you don't have enough cord available, while keeping the strands tight in the anticipated direction of pull.

D. This creates a master point.

E. Clipping into the master point connects you to all the anchors.

quick to tie and easy to adjust (see appendix 2). Always cinch the knot tight and leave tails at least 10 centimeters (4 inches) long. A double grapevine knot as shown here (or triple grapevine, if the cord manufacturer recommends it) is a little stronger; use one of these knots if you expect a high load on the cord, for example if you're using a single loop of cordelette for lead protection.

SELF-EQUALIZING ANCHORS

The idea of self-equalizing is to split the force equally between the pieces, with the

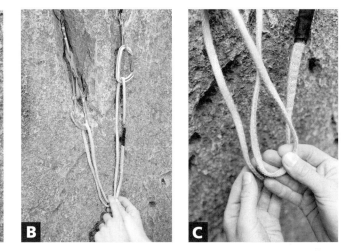

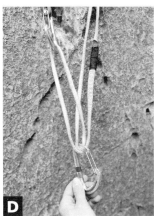

A self-equalizing arrangement allows the clipping carabiner to slide toward the direction of pull and divide the load evenly between the anchors. If the anchors are equalized with a shoulder-length sling (one that fits nicely when placed over-the-shoulder), the extension will not be large if one anchor fails.
A. Clip the sling into both anchors.
B. Pull two strands of sling down between the anchors.
C. Put a 180-degree twist in one of the strands.
D. Clip into both loops to equalize the load.

ability to adjust to different directions of pull. The sliding X is quick and convenient, and with the new thin, low friction Dyneema (Spectra) slings, it spreads the load fairly evenly among the pieces. The equalizer splits the load even more precisely because you don't have the friction of the sliding X running through the carabiner.

Any self-equalizing system extends somewhat if an anchor fails. If you allow too much extension in the rigging and an anchor blows, the fall gets longer. This can create extra impact force on the remaining anchors, and the moving anchor point could force the belayer to lose control of the rope. You can limit the extension to a few inches by tying extension-limiting knots in the longer legs of the webbing or cord.

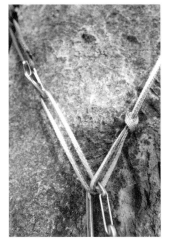

Clipping straight into both strands running between the anchors is dangerous. If one piece fails the whole system will come apart as your carabiner slides off the sling.

If one leg of the self-equalizing sling is long, you can add an extension-limiting knot; this is wise if the anchor attached to the long leg is less-than-bomber. Simply tie an overhand knot in the long leg of the sling above the clipping carabiner. Now, if the anchor attached to the long leg fails, the knot will minimize the sling's extension before the second anchor can catch the load.

If both legs of the sling are long, add two extension-limiting knots to minimize extension in case either anchor fails. With two limiting knots the sliding X becomes a redundant clipping point. Adjust the knots to allow for any possible direction of pull, without allowing too much extension if an anchor blows.

A. If you clip into both strands of webbing between the extension-limiting knots with separate cara-biners you have a redundant tie-in that slides easily to equalize the load.

B. The equalizer worked nicely on Ruper (5.8) in Eldorado Canyon because the previous pitch comes from below and the next pitch traverses right. With this rigging the clipping carabiners can easily slide to adjust to the new pulling direction.

C. Tying the equalizer with two slings makes the clipping loop redundant. This allows you to clip in with a single carabiner which is convenient with larger teams so you don't get too many carabin-ers in the master point.

You can use two slings to make the sliding X redundant. Treat both slings as one as you clip both simultaneously into each an-chor, and twist them together to make the sliding X. This is quick to rig and leaves no welded knots to wrestle with later.

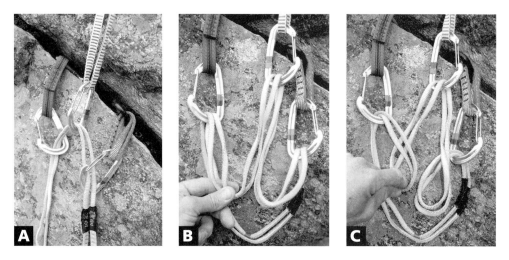

A. You can equalize the load on three or even four pieces with the sliding X. Extend the anchors as necessary to bring the clipping points close together (here the middle piece has been extended with a sling). Two slings are used for redundancy. Clip the slings (preferably made of small diameter Dyneema (Spectra) webbing for less friction) into all three pieces. Treat the slings as one.

B. Pull two loops down between the pieces.

C. Twist an X into both loops.

D. Clip all three loops to equalize the load between the three pieces. Use a large carabiner so the webbing can easily slide to adjust. If one anchor fails, the slack from that loop is split between the other two loops, so extension is minimal.

E. Clipping two or more climbers plus a belay device into all the loops of the sliding X can be tricky. A nice solution is to designate a large locked carabiner as "master carabiner" to function as the master point. Then everyone clips in and out of the master carabiner.

The Trango alpine equalizer makes it easy to equalize the load on a three-point anchor. Simply clip the two outside legs, tie a limiting knot in the middle leg, and clip it. The knot minimizes extension if a piece fails and creates redundancy in the webbing of the equalizer. The knot can also cause all of the force to go onto two pieces rather than three if the loading direction changes.

A. This would usually be extreme overkill, but you can improve the equalization of a cordelette by building a three-loop sliding X on the cordelette legs. Girth hitch a shoulder-length sling to one of the legs just above the tie-off knot, and then clip the sling to the two other legs. A thin-diameter Dyneema (Spectra) sling works best.

B. Pull a loop down between two of the legs and twist a sliding X into each loop.

C. Clip all three loops with a locking carabiner, and clip the cordelette master point with a locker as a backup to the single sling. Keep a little slack between the two tie-ins so the equalizing sling holds the load. This setup will spread the load equally between the anchors, even if the loading direction changes. You'd really only use this rigging if the anchors were mediocre and no other options existed, or possibly if the leader was climbing poorly protected terrain directly above the belay.

V-ANGLE

The V-angle is the angle formed by the legs of the sling or cord. The larger the V-angle, the harder each anchor must pull against the other to hold the downward force. At 60 degrees the force on both anchors is 15 percent greater than the pulling force; at 90 degrees it's 41 percent greater. When you reach 120 degrees the force doubles, and it triples at 141 degrees. At 175 degrees the load multiplies more than 20-fold. For building anchors, a V-angle up to 60 degrees keeps the force reasonable, and an angle of 90 degrees is probably okay for solid anchors.

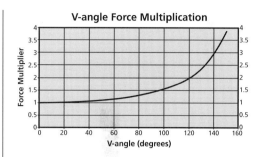

V-angle Force Multiplication

V-ANGLE Graph A.

As the angle formed by the sling or cord increases above 0 degrees, the force on the anchors increases. The increase is moderate at smaller angles.

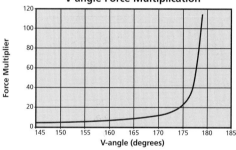

V-angle Force Multiplication

V-ANGLE Graph B.
As the angle approaches 180 degrees, the force explodes.

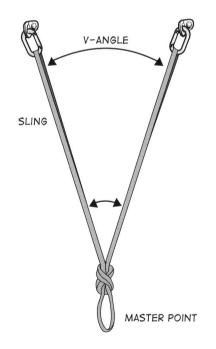

V-ANGLE

SLING

MASTER POINT

Left: The V-angle is the angle between the legs of the sling or cord attached to the anchors.

The relatively shallow V-angle of 55 degrees causes a small increase in the load on the anchors, which will now be about 13 percent greater than the pulling force.

This wide V-angle of about 100 degrees increases the force on the anchors by nearly 60 percent.

PULLEY EFFECT

In a leader fall the top protection must hold the sum of the forces on the climber and the belayer. This is called the pulley

The pulley effect. The top protection gets loaded by the falling climber and the belayer, increasing the load by 60 to 70 percent above the force on the climber.

effect. Friction at the top anchor causes the force on the belayer to be only about two-thirds of the force on the leader, depending on the rope and the carabiner's rope-bearing surface, and assuming that the rope is running clean, with little rope drag. This nearly doubles the impact force on the top anchor beyond the force on the falling climber.

The pulley effect does have a good side: it allows us to create mechanical advantage in hauling systems.

MULTIDIRECTIONAL ANCHORS

In most cases it's beneficial to have a multidirectional belay anchor (one that can handle a pull in any direction) so that a hard leader fall does not lift the belayer *and* the anchors from their perch. If the pitch traverses at the beginning or end, the anchors should also be able to handle a sideways pull.

The first piece of protection in a pitch should be able to handle pulls in the downward or outward direction; otherwise a fall might pop out the first piece, then the second, and so on up the rope. Any lead protection where the rope changes direction should be able to hold both a downward pull and a sideways pull, otherwise that piece may fail during a lead fall.

Bolts, fixed pitons, trees, threads, and well-placed Big Bros are all multidirectional. To some degree, cams set in a parallel placement are multidirectional, because they can swivel to adjust to new loading directions.

Because of the large V-angle between the horizontally-spaced nuts, and the resulting force multiplication be careful trusting this arrangement to catch a hard leader fall. In a vertical crack you don't get the large V-angle, though you get some extra force on the upper piece due to the *pulley effect*: the upper carabiner must hold both the falling climber and the pull from the lower anchor. This effect is diminished by the friction in the sling where it wraps through the carabiner, so the pulley effect should be modest.

CLIMBER ATTACHMENT TO THE ANCHORS

Whenever you're at an exposed belay or rappel station you clip yourself to the anchors. Depending on the situation, you can tie in with the climbing rope, or girth hitch a sling or daisy chain to your harness and clip it to the anchor master point. Clipping with a locking carabiner is best, but you can also substitute two standard carabiners with the gates opposed and reversed. Generally you want to be attached tight to the anchors, without slack in your rope or sling.

OPPOSING NUTS

Wired nuts can oppose each other to create a multidirectional anchor in a horizontal, vertical, or even diagonal crack. One standard way to oppose two nuts is to tie them together on a sling with clove hitches and cinch the clove hitches tight. This method doesn't create active tension, so the nuts don't lock each other in the crack very well. The cinch method shown on the next page creates live tension to hold the nuts in place. You can also set chocks or cams in opposition, or rig a sketchy fixed piton to oppose a good wired nut so the nut doesn't get tugged out of the crack by the rope.

A. Set two opposing nuts about 60 to 100 centimeters (2–3 feet) apart. Clip a sling into one of the nuts, and pass both strands of the sling through a carabiner attached to the other nut.
B. Pass the end of the sling between its own two strands, and again through the carabiner attached to the second nut.
C. Cinch the sling tight to create tension between the two nuts.
D. Clip the sling.

ROPE

If the team is climbing a multipitch route, clip the rope directly to the anchor master point with a locking carabiner for the most secure and convenient attachment. If you're only stopping at the belay briefly to rerack, you may clip to anchors with a sling or daisy chain rather than tying in with the rope.

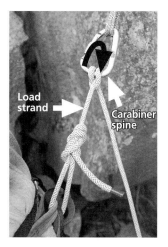

Most guides tie in with a clove hitch because it's easy to adjust, and once you unclip the knot it's gone—nothing left to untie. When belaying a leader, it's wise to set the load strand—the rope strand running to the belayer—close to the carabiner spine (not the gate) to get maximum strength from the carabiner.

The ultra-secure figure eight on a bight makes a good choice for clipping into the anchors.

If a locking carabiner isn't available substitute two standard carabiners. Oppose the gates so they open in opposite directions, and set them both with gates opening down. That way, if one carabiner flips around, one gate opens up while the other opens down to prevent accidental unclipping.

SLING

During rappels the rope is free from the climbing team, so each member needs another method for attaching to the anchors.

A single- or double-length shoulder sling girth-hitched to the harness belay loop or tie-in points makes a convenient loop for clipping the anchors.

Left: Two slings girth-hitched to the harness provide redundancy. Girth hitch them simultaneously (treat two slings as one) to save a step in the setup. You can clip the slings each into a different anchor point as shown, or clip both slings to the anchor master point (usually with a single locking carabiner).

Above: A sewn sling (in good condition) can be girth-hitched to the harness belay loop or tie-in points and clipped to the anchor master point. This is a good way to attach to the anchors on a multi-rappel descent.

Right: A double-length sling (one that fits nicely over the shoulder when doubled) clipped into the anchor gives more extension. You can adjust the effective length of the double sling by tying an overhand knot at the exact length that you desire.

DAISY CHAIN

Daisy chains are almost indispensable for aid climbing on big walls. They allow you to easily clip anchors whether you're tied into the rope or not. Some climbers prefer the simplicity of anchoring with the rope or slings, while others find the convenience of the daisy enticing. Sometimes it depends on the rope system the team is using.

A daisy or sling should not be the sole attachment to the anchors when belaying a leader—the rope should also be connected into the anchors for a bomber attachment.

The daisy chain has many loops so you can easily adjust your extension from the anchors. Most daisy chains load a single bar-tack of stitching at a time, so a high load can begin blowing out the daisy loops.

The dangerous daisy. Never clip more than one daisy loop into a single carabiner; breaking a few loops can cause the daisy to completely unclip from the anchors. This is critically dangerous if two adjacent or nearby loops are clipped into the same carabiner, as shown here. Break a few bar-tacks and you're gone.

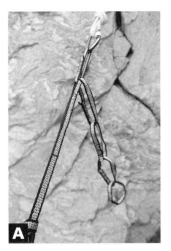

A. The Metolius Personal Anchor System (PAS) is a chain of full-strength loops that provides several attachment lengths. The bomber loops alleviate the problem of bar-tack blow-outs that are possible with a daisy chain. Here the PAS attaches the climber to the anchor master point.

B. A PAS (or daisy chain) can also be used to clip into two bolts. This system doesn't provide any equalization, so it's only good if the bolts are bomber and if the leader isn't likely to fall onto the belay anchors.

Watch your gates! Keep the carabiners oriented so the gates are closed. An open carabiner has only 30 to 45 percent of the strength of a closed one.

BELAYING THE SECOND

Several techniques exist for belaying the second. The "best" technique depends on the situation, the climbing team's preferences, and the quality of the anchors. The rope system or belay techniques of the team may influence the way that they arrange the belay anchors.

DIRECT BELAY

A direct belay with an autoblocking belay device keeps the belayer out of the system. The weight of a falling or hanging climber goes straight onto the anchors, so it's effortless to hold a climber. The direct belay also makes it easy to haul your partner as shown in chapter 5, and to escape the belay in an emergency.

The direct belay only works for belaying the climber(s) following a pitch; it doesn't work for belaying a leader. Autoblocking belay devices currently on the market include the Petzl Reverso and Reversino (for smaller diameter ropes), Trango B-52, Kong GiGi, and Black Diamond ATC Guide.

Make sure you understand the manufacturer's instructions before using one of these devices; they all require specific rigging for autoblocking, plus a special trick for lowering a hanging climber.

The "guide's belay." It's a cinch to belay directly off the anchors with an autoblocking belay device because the belay device automatically locks the rope if the climber falls or hangs. The rope diameter must meet the belay device manufacturer's specifications, and the device must be rigged correctly or the rope may slip rather than lock in a fall.

Guides often clip themselves into the top shelf of the cordelette (the loops coming from each anchor, just above the cordelette's figure eight knot) to keep the master point uncluttered for their partners. Clipping each individual loop connects you to all the anchors. When using the top shelf, first cinch the figure eight tight. If the master point loop is short, put a carabiner in the master point so the knot cannot roll.

Belaying directly off the anchors with a self-locking device like the GriGri can work great. Make sure the cam doesn't press against anything when the GriGri is loaded or it may not engage. The belayer is clipped into the master point here.

For a quick, improvised belay rig a Munter hitch right off the anchors. This works okay for short belays or lowers, but the Munter kinks the rope if you use it for a long length of rope.

Belaying directly off the anchors with a standard belay device is awkward or even dangerous. You need to keep the rope bent across the device to ensure adequate friction in a fall. This belayer also clipped the top shelf incorrectly; she's not actually clipped inside any of the loops, which could be dangerous if an anchor pulled.

REDIRECTED BELAY

If the climber falls or hangs, a redirected belay creates the pulley effect on the anchors: some of the belayer's weight comes onto the anchors to counter the weight of the climber. This increases the load on the anchors, so avoid the redirected belay if the anchors are not bomber. (If the anchors are not great, though, the first choice is to search for better anchors.) In a hanging belay, the belayer's weight is already on the anchors, so redirecting the belay does not increase the force on the anchors.

The redirected belay is used by many climbers because it's easy to hold a hanging climber, and it works with a standard belay device attached directly to the harness. If the climber significantly outweighs the belayer, the belayer should be anchored against an upward pull, or a fall may lift her into the anchors. Here the top shelf provides a strong, redundant point for redirecting.

You can also redirect from a single piece in the belay if the piece is bomber. Don't clip a piece that's too high, though, because a lot of slack will come into the system if that piece fails.

BELAY OFF THE HARNESS

Belaying the second climber off your harness works well if your partner is climbing fast and isn't likely to fall. Belaying off the harness traps you into the system, though, making it uncomfortable to hold a hanging climber and difficult to escape the belay in an emergency. For this reason, many climbers prefer using an autoblocking belay device directly on the anchors.

When belaying off the harness, the belayer should be well-positioned for catching a fall. The acronym ABC describes the lineup: Anchors, Belayer, Climber. The belayer should be in-line between the anchors and the climber, to keep from getting pulled off her stance in a fall.

The belayer is not in line between the anchors and the climber, and she has extra slack in her tie-in. If the climber falls she'll get pulled off her stance and possibly lose control of the rope.

If the belay anchors aren't great, keep looking. If no other options exist, beef them up with a braced leg and good stance. The more parallel your braced leg is to the rope, the better you'll be able to hold a pull. The braced leg anchor is not good for belaying the leader.

BELAYING THE LEADER

When belaying a leader, you'll belay directly off your harness, preferably with the belay device connected to the belay loop.

UPWARD ANCHOR FOR BELAYING

Before belaying a leader, consider whether an upward-pull anchor is important. Belayers often go unanchored when belaying from flat ground. An upward anchor is warranted if:

- the climber is considerably larger than the belayer
- the belay is away from the wall so a fall could slam the belayer into the wall.

An upward-pull anchor that follows the ABC principle will keep you from getting lifted if the leader takes a whipper. Remember though: once you're anchored you are a sitting duck for falling rocks; do it in a safe area.

When belaying on a multipitch climb anchors are mandatory (except—possibly— on the first pitch). Most of the anchors are set for a downward pull, with the belayer positioned below the anchors. A hard fall can still lift the belayer, unless a specific upward anchor is set to prevent this. It's often good for the belayer to lift a bit in a fall because it gives a more dynamic belay, decreasing the force on the climber and the top anchor. It's not good for the belayer to get lifted if she smashes into a roof or another rock feature, so use a direct upward-pull anchor when dangerous features exist.

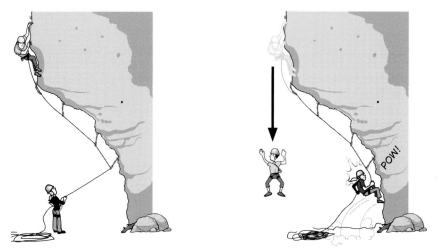

Never belay a leader while standing far away from the wall, or off to the side of the first protection piece, unless you're anchored. Otherwise, if the leader falls she might drag you into the wall, causing her to fall farther, and possibly causing you to lose control of the belay rope. Even if you are anchored, belaying far off to the side puts extra slack in the lead rope, causing the leader to fall farther than necessary if she comes off.

An upward-pull anchor can be clipped directly to the belay loop so any force goes right onto the anchor. This will provide a fairly static belay, but can be useful for small climbers belaying large climbers.

You can use the rope to connect to an upward-pull anchor. Clove hitch the master point, cinch it tight, and then clove hitch the upward anchor and cinch the clove hitches tight against each other. The rigging here will allow some belayer lift, but not much.

You can connect the upward anchor to the back of your harness using a girth-hitched sling, as shown here. You can also clip the anchor to your haul loop, provided it is full-strength.

An upward-pull ground anchor may be warranted when top-roping if the climber seriously outweighs the belayer, or if the belayer is likely to get pulled sideways. Don't do this in a place where rock fall is possible.

ROCK TYPE AND ROCK QUALITY

Good rock quality is critical for setting strong climbing anchors—no anchor can be stronger than the rock it's set in. The strength of the rock depends on the rock type and the condition of the rock surrounding the anchor. Is it solid, fractured, or rotten? An experienced climber automatically assesses rock quality before setting an anchor (or pulling on a hold). Large blocks and flakes can be particularly misleading—big does not necessarily mean solid. If you set an anchor behind a loose flake or block, you could pull the rock off with you in a fall.

Many different rock types exist in the thousands of climbing areas in the world. Granite (and granite-like variations), sandstone, and limestone are the three most prevalent rock types for climbing. Good solid granite provides an excellent medium for rock anchors because the rock is usually strong and solid. Even in good granite, though, you need to beware of rotten or fractured areas. For example, Yosemite granite is impeccably solid in many areas, but you can definitely find bad rock there.

Sandstone varies in quality from super hard and strong, to so soft that it disintegrates like sugar when touched. Fortunately, looking at and touching the rock (and sometimes hitting and kicking it) will provide an assessment of how solid the rock is. Some sandstone has a patina of mineral-hardened rock on the surface, such as the Wingate sandstone in Indian Creek, Utah, and the Aztec sandstone in Red Rocks, Nevada. This patina makes the rock surface harder and stronger, but it can mask underlying soft rock. When a cam gets heavily loaded in this type of rock the cam lobes can punch through the patina into the softer rock and then slide out of the crack, leaving a set of "cam tracks" on each side of the crack. For this reason it's wise to place protection frequently in soft sandstone.

Limestone is fun to climb because it's so featured, but it generally doesn't fracture cleanly like granite or sandstone. This can make it difficult to set removable anchors, which explains why most limestone climbing areas are bolted. When you do set protection anchors in limestone, the crack surfaces are often convoluted, so take care that the anchor sits well in the crack. Sometimes the best option is to set protection in the pockets that are prevalent in limestone.

Dozens of other rock types create a good medium for climbing. It's wise to judge the rock quality for climbing and anchoring before committing to a route, and to continually reassess as you climb.

EXERCISE—BUILDING ANCHOR STATIONS

Set three anchors relatively close together. Practice rigging the following arrangements:

- pre-equalized two-piece anchor with a double sling
- pre-equalized three-piece anchor with a cordelette
- sliding X with a shoulder-length sling
- sliding X with two extension limiting knots
- three-loop sliding X
- equalizer
- opposing nuts
- direct belay with an autolocking device
- redirected belay
- belay off harness with a rope tie-in

SHOCK LOADING

Many climbers and climbing instructors misuse the term "shock loading" to describe the extra-high impact that develops if, as a result of anchor failure, you get extension in the anchor rigging. While you do want to avoid excessive extension in your rigging, a little extension will only lead to the fall being slightly longer, thus increasing the force a little bit. There is no truly super-elevated "shock load" when you have a dynamic lead rope in the system.

CHAPTER 2

Francisco Blanco eyeing a bolt on his route Mora Mora (5.13), Tsaranoro Massif, Madagascar

Natural and Fixed Anchors

Let's say you're climbing a route like the classic *Yellow Spur* in Colorado's Eldorado Canyon. You carry a slim rack because the pitches are short and loads of fixed gear exist. You take the easier, right start, and climb with unwavering control to the first piton, fifteen feet up, which is adorned with a loop of ratty nylon webbing. You clip the piton directly with a shoulder-length sling rather than placing any faith in the faded sling. You continue smooth and steady, still unwilling to fall because you don't really trust the old rusted piton. As soon as you can set a good cam you relax. You avoid clipping another piton because it is off to the side and will cause rope drag; instead you set another good cam, which you trust more anyway. At the end of the pitch you anchor to a decent-sized tree, draped with nylon slings from retreating climbers, and call, "off belay!"

The next two pitches offer some natural protection, which you bypass because the rock looks loose. You do sling a rock tunnel above some of the bad rock, though. On the *Yellow Spur's* famous crux arête pitch, you leave the exposed belay and clip a series of old, fixed pitons. None of them looks great, but there are so many pins, all close together, that you feel safe. Higher up you clip a modern, ⅜-inch diameter bolt and you know you have good protection. The next piece, however, is a ¼-inch bolt left from some decades ago. You sure don't trust that one; in fact you don't even clip it. Instead you climb a little higher to another good bolt, and finally an old bent piton that protects the crux moves. You clip the pin, but don't trust it much, and are happy to have a solid bolt not far below. On the final pitch you wrap the top of the arête with a long sling to protect the second climber, and then traverse to the route's exit.

As on the *Yellow Spur*, many traditional routes have a combination of natural, fixed, and climber-set anchors for protection and belay anchors. It's actually fun being creative and using many different types of anchors to protect your climb.

This chapter discusses natural and fixed anchors including the following:

- trees
- boulders
- blocks
- flakes
- chockstones
- horns and spikes
- threads
- pitons
- bolts

Natural anchors are often quick and easy to rig, and they require only a sling or cord and a carabiner, saving your chocks and cams for other placements. A climber needs to use common sense about what's strong enough—a tied-off branch or loose flake doesn't make a strong anchor, but an obviously solid feature can make a bomber anchor. This chapter will discuss the different types of natural anchors, how to evaluate them, and how to sling them.

The fixed hardware found on many cliffs runs the gamut from perfectly solid to unpredictable to obviously bad. Fortunately, motivated climbers have made a push in recent years to replace most of the old bolts and many of the fixed pitons, but plenty of sketchy fixed gear still exists. Here we'll discuss how to evaluate pitons, and how to discern between good, modern bolts, and old, untrustworthy bolts. The end of the chapter also includes a short discussion about fixed chocks and cams, pieces left behind after they got stuck in a crack.

NATURAL ANCHORS

Many natural anchors, including trees, threads, and some well-wedged chockstones, are multidirectional. Boulders, blocks, and flakes can also be multidirectional, depending on how they are slung. Slung horns or spikes, on the other hand, will usually hold only a downward pull.

TREES

Trees are easy to sling, provided you don't have to crawl through gnarly branches to reach the trunk. Before trusting a tree for anchoring, make sure:

- the roots reach deep into cracks in the rock or into a large, deep patch of soil
- the tree has living leaves or conifer needles
- the tree diameter is large enough to inspire confidence

There is no definitive guideline for safe tree diameter because different types of trees have different strengths, and the root structure strongly influences a tree's strength. However, any reasonably large tree that can withstand the high wind loads common in many climbing areas should be very strong.

Climbers often use a single large tree as their sole belay or rappel anchor. The climbing team must make a wise judgment call before placing total faith in the tree. Even though a single tree does not provide redundant anchor, it's a good idea to rig it with redundant webbing or cord.

Above: If the tree is too large to tie off with the available material, you can simply girth-hitch it. Set the sling so that the clipping loop runs almost straight through the opposite loop in the webbing. For belaying or rappelling, use two slings to make the webbing redundant.

Left: To make the sling redundant, pass it around the tree and tie it off with a figure eight or overhand knot. This creates two independent wraps of webbing for redundancy.

This anchor has three big problems: the tree is small and not very strong; the sling should be set near the ground to minimize leverage on this small tree; the girth hitch bends back across itself which drastically increases the stress on the webbing.

If you must use smaller trees for an anchor, use two or more and equalize the load. Set the webbing near the ground to minimize leverage on the tree.

Often you have many smaller trees growing close together; in this case you can tie off the whole lot of them.

RESPECT THE TREES AND PLANTS

We climbers have a duty to respect and protect our natural environment. Heavy climbing traffic around trees can erode the soil or damage a tree's roots and bark. This can ultimately kill the tree and surrounding plants. In many situations it's better to avoid using trees for anchors if other options exist. Trees rooted in shallow soil are especially vulnerable (and maybe not safe anyway). In some areas, fixed anchors have been installed to protect trees from climber traffic.

If you must rappel from a tree, leave a sling rather than feeding the rope directly around the tree. That way, to retrieve the rope you pull it through the sling, or better, the rappel rings or carabiners attached to the sling, rather than across the bark.

In at least one case, crampon damage from ice climbers destroyed the roots and/or soil holding a tree in place. When two climbers used the tree as a rappel anchor, as did many climbers before, the tree came free; the tree and both climbers plummeted to the ground.

BOULDERS AND BLOCKS

Large boulders, blocks, and flakes can make great natural anchors—if they're solid. Sometimes it's difficult to judge the stability of a block or flake. Before trusting the rock feature, look at the contact surfaces where it meets the rock wall or the ledge. If the surface beneath a boulder or block slopes downward, or if the boulder or block rests on debris, or if the boulder is round, it may not be stable. A very large boulder or block that sits flat on a ledge should be pretty strong.

FLAKES

Flakes, even small ones, can make good anchors if they are solidly connected to the wall. Before using a flake as an anchor (or even as a hand- or foothold), inspect it for cracks. If the bottom of the flake is solidly connected to the wall, it may make a good anchor; if the flake's bottom has any cracks, though, don't trust it. A flake that's not well attached can be hazardous. If you use the flake for protection and fall you might pull the whole thing off; now you are falling *and* the flake is falling behind you.

A flake can be a good anchor if it is solidly attached to the wall, and if the sling wraps securely over the flake.

This boulder has been tied off with a cordelette using two independent wraps for redundancy.

When slinging all but the largest flakes, set the webbing or cord near the flake's bottom to minimize leverage on the flake. Be careful that the sling material does not contact sharp edges on the flake. If so, move the sling or add an extra sling for redundancy.

HORNS AND SPIKES

A sling around a solid horn or spike of rock makes a quick, easy anchor—but only for a downward pull. The rock needs to be solid and needs to have a positive lip to hold the sling in place.

This horn makes a good anchor provided that the lead rope does not lift it off the horn.

You can hang a heavy piece (or pieces) of the rack on the sling to help hold it in place.

If the horn is used for lead protection you might tie a slip knot to help hold it in place. This works especially well on chickenheads, which have a bigger diameter at the head of the horn than at the throat (like a chicken's head).

CHOCKSTONES

Chockstones are rocks that have fallen and become wedged into a crack during some eon of time. A chockstone can make a good anchor if it's wedged securely, and if the chockstone and rock walls are solid. Be careful of huge sketchy chockstones that could fall or roll and hurt you. Before trusting a chockstone, *carefully* test it's stability. It's often best to girth-hitch a sling on the edge of the chockstone where it meets the rock wall, so the sling does not roll the chockstone.

This chockstone is slung correctly.

This chockstone is not stable; it can easily roll inside the crack. Worse, the sling is set in a way that will cause the chockstone to roll.

CHOKES AND THREADS

A solid thread will hold a pull in any direction. Estimate the strength of the thread based on the thickness and quality of the rock that supports the sling or cord. Be careful of sharp edges where the sling or cord contacts the rock. If the fit is tight, it can be tricky to feed the sling—a nut tool might help.

Right: You can wrap a sling through a spot where two boulders or other rock features come together.

Sometimes you can thread a natural tunnel in the rock with a sling or piece of cord to create an anchor—limestone is often generous with threading opportunities.

FIXED ANCHORS

Bolts, and sometimes pitons, are fixed in place for all climbers to use, until they rust away or get replaced with new hardware. Occasionally you also find nuts and cams stuck in the crack. Climbs have varying amounts of fixed pro, from trad lines with no fixed gear, to sport climbs protected entirely by bolts. On some traditional routes you'll clip the occasional bolt, piton, or stuck piece for protection. A *mixed* route may have several bolts, with some sections requiring nuts or cams for protection.

Fixed anchors can be totally solid, completely sketchy, or anywhere in between. It's up to you to understand the various types of fixed gear, especially what's bomber and what's not. Using this information helps you inspect fixed gear to judge how solid it is.

PITONS

On July 4, 1893, William Rogers pounded wooden wedges up the basalt cracks to build a ladder to the summit of Devils Tower in Wyoming. These are still in place, but you wouldn't want to climb on them anymore. Soon thereafter climbers started using soft steel pitons. They were stronger than the wooden wedges previously used, but they deformed with use and quickly became trashed. In the 1960s Yvon Chouinard developed hard steel pitons that could be driven and removed repeatedly. These were used to pioneer scores of early free and aid routes. You still find old fixed pitons scattered around in many traditional climbing areas.

Fixed pitons can be helpful, especially in sections where the route has no cracks big enough to accept chocks or cams. The problem is, it can be difficult to judge how solid a fixed piton is: it might be totally bomber, or pitifully weak.

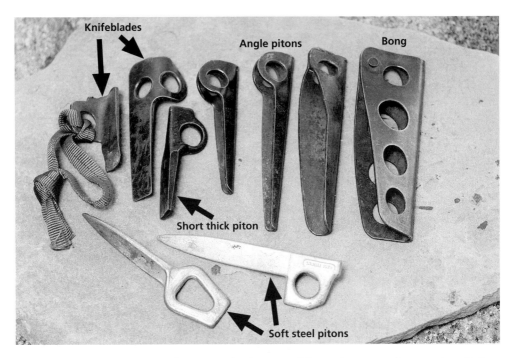

One of the keys to a solid piton placement is having a good fit, so pitons come in many sizes. Knifeblades can be bomber or sketchy. The problem is, when they're fixed you can't tell how long they are, or how corroded. Knifeblades range from 1.3 millimeters (0.05 inches) to 3.2 millimeters (.13 inches) thick. Angle pitons are bent midway along their long axis so they fit wider cracks. They come in several sizes to fit cracks from 1.3 to 4 centimeters (½- to 1 ½-inches). Big cams have made bongs nearly obsolete, but you still find a few out on the cliffs. If the clipping eye is damaged you can sling the bong like a chockstone.

Before trusting a fixed piton, visually inspect the rock, the placement, and the piton's condition to learn as much as you can. Tap the piton with a carabiner if you want to learn more: a hollow thud means it's not well set, while a high-pitched ring means it's sitting tight. Inspect the piton for rust or other signs of corrosion, cracks, and structural damage; but remember, the worst corrosion is often inside the crack,

where it's impossible to see. If you're uncertain, back up the pin with a good cam or nut if possible.

Sometimes fixed pitons are superfluous, set in a crack that easily accepts chocks or cams. In these situations it's often better to set your own protection, or to clip the piton as well as your own gear. Occasionally you can use a fixed piton to help prevent a nut from being wriggled free by the climbing rope.

Pitons can be tough to evaluate. This piton in a vertical crack may be long or short, new or corroded, you can't tell.

A piton set in a horizontal crack can be better than one in a vertical crack because it will cam inside the crack rather than rotate out.

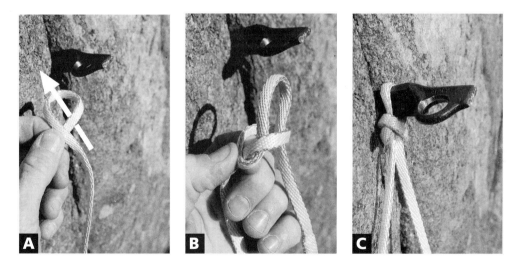

You can increase the strength of some pitons by tying them off to reduce leverage.
A. Make a coil in the webbing.
B. Push the webbing through itself to make a slip knot.
C. Place the slip knot over the head of the piton, slide it flush against the wall, and cinch it tight.

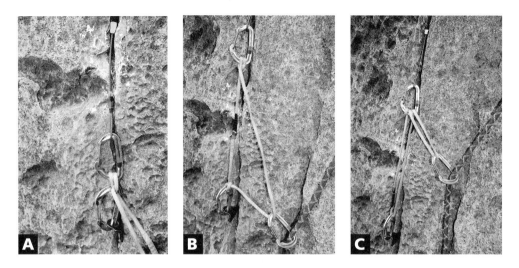

A fixed piton can be rigged to oppose a nut and help hold it in place.
A. If the two pieces are close together, tie their carabiners into the same clove hitch.
B. If the pieces are farther apart, tie them together with two separate clove hitches.
C. You can also tension the piton and nut against one another by opposing them as shown in chapter 1. (Note: This will increase the force on the nut, due to the pulley effect.)

Setting a Piton

To set a piton, find a horizontal or "key-locked" placement. Choose the correct size piton for the crack. If the piton will become fixed protection, drive it home with a hammer until the eye just protrudes from the rock; if your partner will remove it, set the piton just enough for your needs—only bury it if you have to. Listen to the piton as you drive it. A ringing "ping" that increases in pitch as you hammer means the piton is finding a solid home. A dull "thud" means the rock around the piton is rotten or hollow.

BOLTS

John Otto pounded steel rods into drilled holes to make his 1911 ascent of Indepen-

The proliferation of bolts over the last twenty years has allowed many climbing areas and routes to be created that would be unattractive to climbers otherwise.

dence Monument in Colorado National Monument. This gargantuan pioneering effort was among the first that involved drilling holes and setting "bolts" for anchoring on a rock face. Now bolts have proliferated at climbing areas around the world.

Bolts can be a touchy subject. To some climbers a line of bolts is an enticing

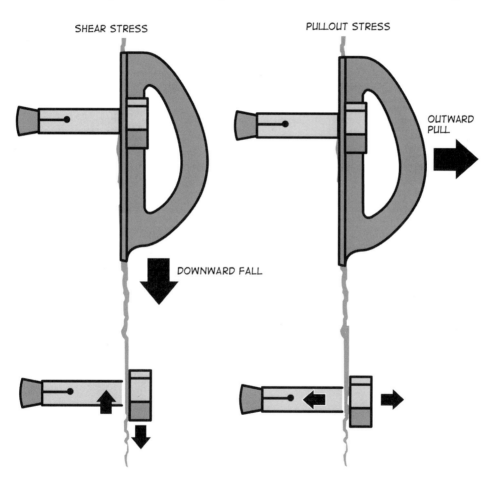

SHEAR STRESS

PULLOUT STRESS

OUTWARD PULL

DOWNWARD FALL

Bolt Stress. A bolt needs high shear strength to resist pulls perpendicular to its axis, and good pullout strength to resist forces along the bolt's axis. A fall on a vertical wall or slab creates mostly shear stress on the bolt, though a climber who pitches outward in a fall will also create some pullout force. A team hanging at an anchor station and leaning out creates both shear and pullout stress on the anchors. A bolt set in a horizontal roof will receive mostly pullout stress if the climber falls or hangs on the bolt.

vertical path; to others bolts are an eyesore, an example of poor climbing style, or even an environmental travesty. When bolted sport climbs first came onto the American climbing scene in the 1980s, the ensuing bolt wars divided the climbing community. Bolts were placed, chopped, replaced, and re-chopped, and friends became enemies. The real loser was the rock, which is still scarred in some areas. Fortunately most climbers have moved past bolting controversies, though areas of contention still exist.

Most bolts used for climbing in North

The 13-millimeter (½-inch) 5-piece bolts and the 10-millimeter (³⁄₈-inch) wedge bolts make great rock climbing anchors, provided they are properly set in solid rock, and are not rusted or corroded.

America are mechanical bolts originally designed by the construction industry for fastening structures to concrete and stone. The bolts are coupled with a hanger so climbers can clip carabiners to the anchor. Two styles of mechanical bolts are prevalent: the 5-piece bolt and the wedge bolt. Both styles are available in carbon steel, or, for triple the price, stainless steel. Stainless is the better choice in all but the driest climates. To set a mechanical bolt you drill a hole into the rock, blow out the rock dust, fix the bolt with a hanger, and then pound it into the drilled hole. Tightening the bolt expands it inside the hole to provide good shear and pullout strength.

5-piece bolt. Some of the most bomber bolts you'll find are often called 5-piece bolts. Powers Fasteners (formerly Rawl) distributes these under the name "Power-Bolt." The actual bolt screws through a metal sleeve into a cone-shaped expander. To set a 5-piece bolt, pound the bolt assembly into the drilled hole. Tightening the bolt pulls the expander cone into the metal sleeve, which expands the sleeve. Further tightening pushes the end of the bolt through the expander cone, which expands its four sections to undercut the rock near the base of the hole. This gives the bolt tremendous pullout strength. The bolt itself can actually be unscrewed and removed, while the sleeve and expander remain fixed in the hole.

Wedge bolt. Wedge bolts are available from Powers, Petzl, and Fixe. They are somewhat easier to place than 5-piece bolts, especially when set on lead. Tightening a wedge bolt pulls the wedge cone into the expansion cylinder, which expands to lock the bolt in the hole.

Glue-in. Glue-in bolts are abundant in some areas and rare in others. They are the best choice for sea cliffs and corrosive rock (some limestone contains elements that rapidly corrode bolts). The one-piece bolt and hanger design prohibits the galvanic corrosion that occurs between dissimilar metals (as in a standard bolt with a separate hanger),

BAD BOLTS

The bolts shown here were commonly used to protect climbs from the 1950s through the 1980s. Several groups have launched noble efforts to replace these dangerous bolts with modern ones, but plenty of old bolts can still be found in some climbing areas. They are not trustworthy: they're too thin, too short, and most have been sitting in the cliff for two to five decades.

Bolts in marine climates are especially susceptible to corrosion, as are bolts in wet limestone. In some cases, bolts as new as three years failed under mere body weight. The culprit seems to be the salty air and sea spray, combined with corrosive minerals from the rock (some limestone seems to be particularly bad). The process is accelerated in sunny areas with high temperatures. Unfortunately, the corrosion may not be visually obvious.

Don't trust bolts that are:
- smaller than 10-millimeters (³⁄₈-inch) in diameter
- rusty or corroded (some forms of corrosion are invisible)
- loose
- set in bad rock
- equipped with a funky homemade hanger

The 6.5-millimeters (¼-inch) diameter wedge bolt, 6.5-millimeters (¼-inch) buttonhead, and 10 millimeter (³⁄₈-inch) Star Dry bolts are outdated and unsafe.

This sea cliff bolt is totally rusted and untrustworthy. Some corrosion on sea cliffs and limestone is invisible and impossible to detect.

plus the glue can provide a barrier between the rock and the bolt. The epoxy that glues the bolt into the hole gives it great pullout strength—provided the epoxy is applied correctly. Most glue-in bolts are stainless steel. The most corrosion-resistant of all bolts is the titanium Tortuga glue-in, which was designed specifically for use on sea cliffs.

Hangers

The basic bolt hanger is a stamped piece of stainless steel with a 90-degree bend. One side of the bend has a hole for the bolt, and the other is cutout for clipping. A good hanger has the edges of the cutout rounded so they don't gouge carabiners.

Welded cold shuts are versatile because you can clip them like any bolt hanger, or run your rope directly through the hanger for rappelling. The cold shut needs a high quality weld to have adequate strength for climbing. Unwelded cold shuts will hold body weight but may bend open and let you down in a leader fall.

Standard bolt hanger

FIXED CHOCKS AND CAMS

Often you'll find stuck nuts and cams, especially on popular classic routes. As long as the sling is not faded and stiff, and the piece is not mangled, a fixed piece can be "reasonably" trustworthy—it's up to you to inspect the fixed gear and decide how much to trust it. Clip the cable directly, if possible, to avoid trusting an old sling. A kind leader informs her partner that the gear is fixed if it's not obvious, so that the second climber doesn't waste energy and psyche battling to clean a fixed piece.

EXERCISE—NATURAL ANCHORS

On your next few climbs, seek out natural anchors, whether you're leading or setting top-rope or belay anchors. Find the natural protection that makes sense and incorporate it into your protection system. Some climbing areas offer more natural protection opportunities than others.

If you can retrieve a fixed nut or cam, it's your prize to keep. Some climbers have entire racks made of booty. Since you don't know the history, though, it's better not to trust found gear too much. If you decide to climb with the booty, at least inspect the gear closely and replace slings or cords.

CHAPTER 3

Silvia Luebben setting a nut on Max Factor (5.11c), Vedauwoo, Wyoming

Chocks

One of the Eastern centers of traditional climbing, the Shawangunks in New York, was discovered for rock climbing by Fritz Weissner in the 1930s. He soon opened a number of routes up to 5.7, a respectable difficulty given the era and the primitive gear. *Modern Times* is one of the classics opened in the 1960s. It follows the typical horizontally banded quartz conglomerate, busting through big roofs on big holds.

You definitely want a good selection of cams on *Modern Times*; they work best when the horizontal cracks are parallel, and when you need to set the gear quickly. But you'll also carry wired nuts and possibly some Tri-cams or hexes. These give a bomber placement in spots where the crack wavers, and where the horizontal cracks are lipped. They also work at the belay, so you can save the precious cams for the lead.

This chapter covers all the types of protection other than cams, including:

- wired nuts
- micronuts
- hexes
- Tri-cams
- slider nuts
- Big Bros

For each type of anchor we discuss:

- pros and cons
- how to set and remove it
- how to evaluate the placement

Technically Tri-cams and Big Bros are cams because of the way they transfer a downward pulling force into a horizontal force against the crack walls, but they are included here so spring-loaded camming units can have their own chapter. Most of the chocks might also be considered *passive protection,* because they have no moving parts. Cams and slider nuts fall into the *active protection* category because the spring actively holds the protection in place. Expandable tube chocks have moving parts and a spring, and they are held in the crack by pressure from the locking collar, so they are also active protection.

EVOLUTION OF CLIMBING CHOCKS

Pitons were the predominant climbing anchors for many years. Each piton placement chipped some rock away, though; in time the popular routes became pitifully scarred. Years later you can still find these piton scars on the old classic routes. In fact, the scars create the finger jams and pockets on many modern free climbs.

British climbers began the movement toward "clean climbing" that required no hammer and did not scar the rock. They started by tying slings around chockstones for protection. As early as 1926, some clever Brits stuffed their pockets with stones to jam in the crack and tie off for protection. Eventually they scavenged machine nuts along the railroad tracks, filed out the threads, and slung the holes with cord. Soon enough they were drilling holes in the larger nuts to save weight.

Some of the first commercially available climbing nuts, first manufactured in Great Britain in the 1960s, on display at the Neptune Mountaineering climbing museum in Boulder, Colorado

Armed with racks of machine nuts, they tackled increasingly difficult climbs. In the early 1960s they began making nuts specifically for climbing. They experimented with many exotic shapes: truncated cones, pyramids, knurled cylinders, and T- and H-shaped bars. Ultimately, the wedge and hexagonal shapes emerged as the most practical due to their good stability and high strength-to-weight ratio.

Most climber's resisted clean climbing—at first. They trusted their pitons, and they weren't going to trust a chunk of metal slotted in a crack. Pitons probably would have held their ground, except that slotting nuts is much easier than banging pitons. Once climbers realized this, they dumped their heavy hammers and iron for light nuts and hex-shaped chocks made of aircraft aluminum.

The most versatile nut, the Tri-cam, was invented by Greg Lowe in 1973, and came to market in 1981. Tri-cams are unique because they can jam in a constriction like a wedge, or cam in a parallel crack. Tri-cams have a cult of followers who always carry a few small Tri-cams. They swear by Tri-cams, while others swear at them. Tri-cams work great in many situations, but the larger sizes never caught on because they lack the stability of spring-loaded cams. There's nothing worse than having your protection fall out well below your feet.

Friends, the first commercially successful cams, appeared in 1978. As cams took over, larger chocks (bigger than finger-size) took the back seat. A climber might carry large chocks, but only to supplement a set or two of cams. Wired nuts have held their

ground, though. They remain the warhorse for protecting thin cracks.

Climbers experimented with sliding nuts, double wedges sliding against one another to lock in a crack (similar to the way a door stop works) as early as 1946. Finally, in 1983 they became available when Doug Phillips introduced Sliders. The design was improved by Steve Byrne with his Ball Nutz, which have a ball that rotates in a groove to accommodate mildly flaring cracks.

The author designed Big Bro expandable tube chocks, with help from Chuck Grossman and mechanical engineering professor Jaime Cardenas-Garcia, in 1984. The name comes from George Orwell's book *1984*, and the line "Big Brother is watching you." Big Bros came to market in 1987, extending protection into the realm of off-widths and squeeze chimneys—anything from 8 to 30.5 centimeters (3.2 to 12 inches). The range grew with two new sizes added in 2003 that extend the coverage from 7 to 47 centimeters (2.7 to 18.4 inches). Almost any crack can be protected now; the limiting factor is the skill, strength, and determination of the climber.

WIRED NUTS

Wired nuts are indispensable on many traditional climbs. They work wonders jamming in the constrictions of small, irregular cracks. Because they are small and light, you can carry a bunch of them. They're cheap, too, at least compared to cams. Losing some wired nuts to bail off a route won't leave you crying.

A set of well-used wired nuts

Wired nuts come in many sizes, ranging from 3.8 to 50 millimeters (0.15 to 2.0 inches). They work great in the small to medium sizes, but hexagonal chocks or Tri-cams may be a better choice for "passive" protection (pro with no moving parts) for cracks wider than 25 millimeters (1 inch).

SETTING NUTS

When seeking a spot in the crack to set a nut, look for:

▪ **Solid rock surrounding the nut**. Fractured, rotten, friable, or soft rock may shatter under load.
▪ **Constrictions** that jam the nut against a downward pull, and ideally against an outward tug, too.
▪ **A good fit**. Choose the right size of nut to best fit the crack. If the nut doesn't fit well, try the next size. If you're setting a curved nut, orient the concave face to the right or left so it best fits the crack, striving for maximum surface contact between the nut and the rock.

Think **R**ock **DOG**:

▪ The **R**ock must be solid;
▪ The crack should have constrictions to oppose a **D**ownward pull, and ideally an **O**utward pull;
▪ The nut should have a **G**ood fit in the crack.

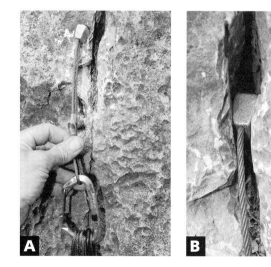

A. Look for a spot where the crack keylocks the nut. Slide the nut through the bigger area of the crack. Usually you'll do this with the nut still attached to the carabiner full of nuts. This allows you to try another size if the first nut doesn't fit well.
B. Nestle it down into a stable placement and clip it.

A bomber nut placement resists both a downward and an outward pull, and has good surface contact with the rock.

To Tug or Not to Tug. If the nut fits well you can usually just place it gently in the crack. Your partners will appreciate it. Sometimes a light tug helps set your nut. Occasionally it's wise to set the nut with a sharp tug (or a few). If the placement doesn't have a good lip to resist an outward pull and you can't find a better spot, or if you're runout and absolutely need the nut to stay in place, then go ahead and yank it. Save this bullying technique for crucial times, though; your partners will hate cleaning a pitch full of yanked, stuck nuts.

CLEANING NUTS

To remove a nut, imagine the path it took going into the crack. Usually it's obvious,

You can push, prod, poke or pull with a nut tool to liberate stubborn nuts. Rig the nut tool with a keeper cord that stays clipped to your harness or a shoulder sling so you can't drop the nut tool.

For bigger nuts, you can lever them with the hooking end of the nut tool to get them moving.

If the nut refuses to budge, hold the working end of the nut tool against the stuck nut and smack the other end with a large chock. You can also use a fist-sized rock to hit the nut tool, but be careful not to drop it.

but sometimes the nut was wriggled through some intricate maze that must be retraced to free the piece. Hold the cables and try to wriggle the nut loose, then work it out through the opening. If it won't budge you might try whipping the cable upwards with the carabiner to loosen it; overusing this practice will bend and eventually fray a nut's cables, and it also might get the nut more stuck.

Sometimes a nut gets really stuck, especially if the leader fell or hung, or set it with a yank. If the nut won't budge, break out the nut tool.

SHAPE AND FIT

A good fit maximizes the surface contact area between the nut and the rock, decreasing the pressure on the rock and adding strength and stability to the placement. Nuts are available in different shapes to help you find the best fit for a given crack. Curved nuts have a concave face on one side and a convex face on the other; they fit securely in many tapering placements, and are the favorites of many climbers. Straight-sided nuts have no curve, but they fit many cracks well, and they get stuck less than curved nuts. Offset nuts fit flared cracks and piton scars, making them especially useful for aid climbing and for protection in areas with flaring cracks and piton scars.

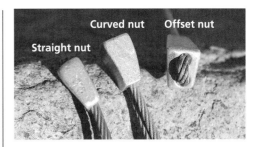

Straight-sided, curved, and offset nuts

Often climbers place mediocre protection that could be much better with just a minor adjustment—sometimes moving the piece only a few millimeters vastly improves the placement. Pay special care to find the best fit.

This nut might fit better, with more surface contact, if it was turned the other way. As it is, it has poor surface contact on the right side and nothing to hold it against an outward pull.

This nut has poor contact on the left side. If just a little rock breaks, it's outta' there!

This endwise nut has poor surface contact on the right side. It's likely to fall out of the crack with a little wriggle from the rope.

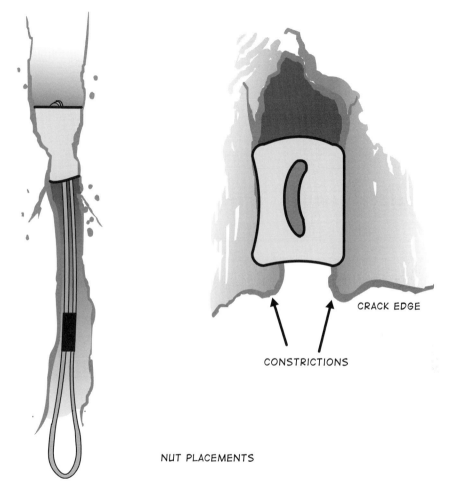

SIDE VIEW

TOP VIEW

CRACK EDGE

CONSTRICTIONS

NUT PLACEMENTS

If you can find downward and outward constrictions and fit them with the right size nut, you'll have a secure placement.

In a pinch you can set a nut endwise to fit a bigger crack, but it's not as secure as a sideways placement because you get less surface contact.

In a horizontal crack, try to find an opening in the back of the crack that allows you to slide the nut towards a constriction on the edge of the crack. Such a placement can be bomber. The piece shown is good provided it does not get pulled to the left.

The crack has no constriction to resist an outward pull, so the rope may wriggle the nut out, or the nut might pop out in a fall. Even worse, it has very poor surface contact with the rock. If the rock breaks a little, the nut will fail.

This nut could pull the fractured block on the left side loose. Be careful what you set your anchors behind. The nut also relies on a thin, fractured layer on the right side.

MICRONUTS

Micronuts fit the tiniest cracks, but they have limited strength—the nuts, wires, and contact area with the rock are small. The smallest micronuts are intended for aid placements only, or perhaps to oppose a larger nut and hold it in place. In a good placement in solid rock, larger micronuts can be strong enough to catch *most* falls.

Traditional micronuts are made of brass, with a stainless steel cable silver-soldered to the nut. The soldering avoids a sharp bend in the cable and fills the holes drilled for inserting the cable, which maximizes the strength of the small nut. Some micronuts are made of copper-infused steel, which provides strength and grip with the rock surface.

Micronuts fill the void for tiny cracks. Here we have some classic RPs, HB Offsets, and Metolius Astronuts.

The placement looks pretty good for a micronut. Still, it's a good idea to back up small placements.

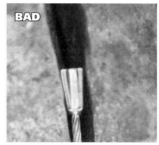

This placement doesn't have good surface contact on the right side.

This nut is too close to the edge of the crack, and it's barely touching on the left side.

This nut has poor surface contact on the right side. A slight outward tug in a fall or a little rope wriggle will free this micronut from the crack.

83

EQUALIZING THE LOAD

When setting micronuts or small wired nuts, consider setting two and equalizing them so that they share the load to make a stronger anchor.

To get more strength from micronuts or small wired nuts (or other sketchy gear), set two and equalize them with a shoulder-length sling. Don't forget the 180-degree twist in the sling!

In a rare circumstance you can self-equalize three anchors with a sling. Clip the sling into each of the nuts; pull down a loop of sling between each of the three nuts, and put 180-degree twists in two of the loops. Clip all three loops. Though it's time- and gear-consuming, equalizing small or weak protection increases the chances that they will hold.

HEXAGONAL CHOCKS

Chocks based on a modified hexagonal shape work like a normal nut, only they're designed to fit bigger cracks. The four or five sizes ranging from 2.5 to 6.5 centimeters (1- to 2.5- inches) seem the most practical, though you can buy smaller and larger models. Hexagonal chocks come slung with webbing or cable. The webbing is lighter and stronger, while the cable-slung hexes allow you to reach high placements and are less prone to tangling on the rack.

When placing a hex-shaped chock, find a downward constriction to jam the chock, and an outward constriction to hold it in place. Strive for maximum surface contact between the rock and the chock. Hexagonal chocks can cam somewhat in a crack, due to the sling (or cable) position causing a rotation of the chock, but no spring exists to hold the chock in place so they work best when jammed in a constriction. Because of the asymmetric shape you can fit two crack sizes with a sideways placement, and a third size with an endwise placement.

Hexes cover the range from finger cracks to fist cracks.

Far left: A hexagonal-shaped chock set sideways can be bomber. A chock set endwise fits a wider crack. Chocks are significantly lighter than the same-size camming units.

Left: This hex was slipped through an opening into a constriction at the lip of this horizontal crack. It will hold a multidirectional pull.

This hex placement is not stable because it's set too close to the crack edge and there is nothing to hold it against an outward pull. Also the rock is grainy on the right side, and the surface contact on that side is spotty.

SLINGING CHOCKS

Most chocks and camming units come with a sewn webbing sling or swaged cable loop for clipping. Some commercial outfits replace worn slings, or you can tie on your own when the sling gets worn. Use climbing webbing or cord with a strength rating of at least 16 kN (3600 pounds) for reslinging the gear. Tie cord into a loop with a double fisherman's, unless the cord manufacturer recommends a triple fisherman's, and tie webbing with a water knot. Check your water knots each time you use them, as they tend to untie with repeated loading.

TRI-CAMS

Climbers love or hate Tri-cams, often based on where they climb. Tri-cams are extremely versatile, with two placement modes: you can wedge a Tri-cam in a tapering crack just like a nut, or cam it in a parallel crack. Their compact shape allows them to fit in pockets or pods where nothing else can.

Eleven sizes cover cracks from 1.6 to 14 centimeters (.63 to 5.5 inches), but the smallest four sizes are the most useful. The biggest Tri-cams can be unstable—a little rope movement can wriggle them out of the crack.

Tri-cams come in eleven sizes but the smallest sizes are the most useful.

When wedging a Tri-cam, find a fit that gives good surface contact between the Tri-cam and the rock with a good constriction to hold the Tri-cam in place.

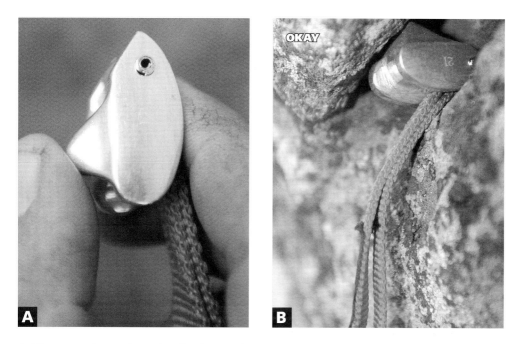

A. When camming a Tri-cam, lay the sling inside the rails.

B. Set the fulcrum (or point) in a divot, micro crack, or small edge inside the crack or pocket for stability. Tug the Tri-cam to set it, and be careful not to wriggle it loose with the rope. This placement would be better if the fulcrum were sitting in a tiny divot rather than on a flat face.

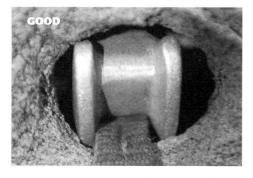

Sometimes Tri-cams work where nothing else will, like in this small pocket.

This Tri-cam is unstable because it's in a flaring pocket, and because the fulcrum has no rock feature to hold it in place.

SLIDING NUTS

Sliding nuts fit parallel cracks from 3 to 16 millimeters (.12 to .63 inch). On these Trango Ball Nutz, the semispherical "ball" wedges against the "ramp" like a door on a door stop. This creates a large outward force that generates friction to oppose a pull. The ball can rotate to adjust for a small amount of flare in the crack. A small camming unit is usually more reliable than a sliding nut.

Sliding nuts work in tiny parallel cracks where nothing else fits except wired nuts that could slide out.

To set a ball nut:

A. *Retract the trigger and insert the piece in a crack, just above a minor constriction in the crack if possible. Release the trigger so the ball jams against the ramp. It should be 50 percent or less expanded and have good surface contact with the rock for maximum security. Tug the ball nut to test it and set it.*

B. *This placement looks reasonably good. The piece was extended with a quickdraw (not shown) so the rope wouldn't wriggle the ball nut free.*

Left: If you set a ball nut in a less-than-perfect placement, consider setting two and equalizing them.

EXPANDABLE TUBES

Big Bro expandable tubes cover cracks from 7 to 47 centimeters (2.6 to 18.4 inches). A Big Bro is much lighter and more compact than a giant cam, and more stable when set in a good placement. You can't slide the Big Bro up the crack like a cam, though. A big cam is easier to set than a Big Bro and works better in flared cracks.

Six sizes of Big Bro expandable tubes protect parallel cracks from fist cracks to small chimneys. Big Bros are lighter and more compact than giant camming units, but harder to place.

Big Bros provide anchors in the offwidths and squeeze chimneys that most climbers hate to climb, such as Texas Finger Crack (5.11), Escalante Canyon, Colorado.

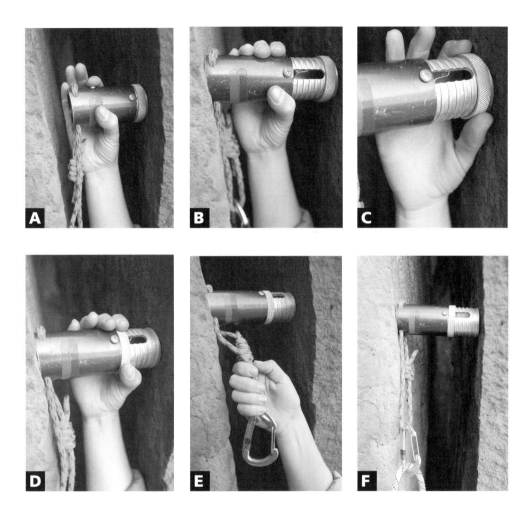

To place a Big Bro:

A. Find a parallel spot in the crack and push the inner tube against the crack wall.

B. Push the trigger so the tube expands to fit the crack. Don't "dry-fire" a Big Bro by pushing the button and letting the inner tube slam against the stop—instead, let the tube expand slowly.

C. With the spring holding the tube in place, spin the locking collar.

D. Crank the collar down tight.

E. Tug sharply on the Big Bro's sling to test the stability. Retighten the collar.

F. Clip the rope to the sling using a carabiner.

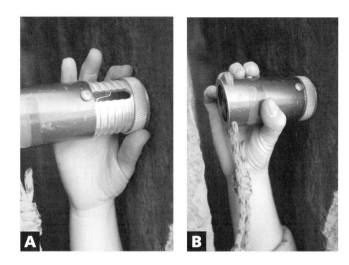

A. To remove a Big Bro, spin the collar to the end of the tube.
B. Collapse the unit until the trigger pops up.

If the crack flares, find the most parallel placement possible. Set the slung end so it fully contacts the rock, and let the other side touch in one point like a Tri-cam. Use a long sling so the rope doesn't disturb the placement, and be careful not to knock it loose as you climb past.

The new 3.8-centimeter (1.5 inch) diameter mini Big Bros, available in sizes 0.5 and 1, are extremely light and compact. They are great for saving weight on long stretches of fist cracks (mix them in with some big cams), or on alpine climbs.

SIZE AND STRENGTH

All brands and models of chocks come in a set of complementary sizes, from small to large, and are numbered according to size.

This creates a selection for fitting various cracks: if a piece is too small, try the next bigger size.

It's wise to not trust the tiniest nuts much; even if the nut doesn't break, the rock might. A small nut might slow you down, though, or stop a short fall, especially if you're high up on the pitch so the impact force is low. To increase the odds of nuts holding, consider equalizing two small nuts.

Only nuts bigger than 8 to 14 millimeters thick (.3 to .55 inch), depending on the brand, rate a full strength of 10 or 12 kN (2250 to 2700 pounds), which is sufficient to hold most climbing falls. In these medium and larger sizes, rock quality and placement stability become the important factors for ensuring placement security. One brand of hexagonal chocks rates below full strength in the smallest two sizes (rated 6 kN/1350 pounds), but most of brands rate from 10 to 14 kN (2250 to 3150 pounds) throughout the size range.

The smallest two Tri-cams rate slightly below full strength (8.2 and 8.8 kN/1845 and 1980 pounds), but the larger Tri-cams have the highest published strength of any chocks—up to 20 kN (4500 pounds). Sliding nuts are not as strong, ranging from 4.5 to 8 kN (1000 to 1800 pounds), depending on the size. Because of their limited strength and fickle nature, use these devices with care. Expandable tubes rate a burly 15 kN (3375 pounds) across their size range.

	SIZE (APPROX. WIDTH)		STRENGTH	
	mm	(inches)	kN	(pounds)
Wired nuts	3.8	.16	2	450
	5	.20	4-5	900-1125
	6	.24	4-6	900-1350
	7	.28	6-7	1350-1575
	8	.32	6-12	1350-2700
	9	.35	6-12	1350-2700
	10	.40	6-12	1350-2700
	12	.47	6-12	1350-2700
	14-50	.55-2.0	10-12	2250-2700
Total size range	3.8-50	.16-2.0		
Hexagonal chocks	10	.42	6-10	1350-2250
	14	.55	10	2250
	25-89	1.0-3.5	10-14	2250-3150
Total size range	10.6-89	.42-3.5		
Tri-cams	16	.63	8.2	1845
	19	.75	8.8	1980
	25	1.0	11.1	2500
	32	1.25	13.3	3000
	41	1.62	17.7	3980
	57-140	2.25-5.5	20	4500
Total size range	16-140	.63-5.5		
Sliding nuts	3	.12	4.5	1000
	6-16	.24-.63	8	1800
Total size range	3-16	.12-.63		
Big Bros	69-467	2.7-18.4	15	3375
Total size range	69-467	2.7-18.4		

The chart shows the strengths published by various manufacturers for different sizes of chocks. When the strength rating shows a range, it means that some brands are stronger in that size than others. The size listed is the approximate dimension for the thickness (smallest width) of the chock (a nut has two sizes, while a hexagonal chock has three; the listed size is the smallest of these).

EXERCISE—GEAR PLACEMENT

New Trad Climber:

Round up an assortment of nuts and chocks, as well as some Tri-cams, slider nuts, and Big Bros. Find a cliff base with good cracks and no climbers above and set all the different sizes of nuts and chocks. Find placements that keylock the pieces in the crack so they cannot get pulled out. Clip a sling to the pieces and yank on them to test their stability. Pull down, and also yank them outward to see if they can handle that direction of pull.

Set lots of different pieces, and try to pick the right size on the first try. Notice how a piece is much more stable with good rock surface contact, and how a curved nut sometimes fits better if you turn it to face the other way.

Intermediate Trad Climber:

This exercise is also a personal challenge. Go to the cliff base with wired nuts and chocks and set some pieces. Before choosing which nut to set in the crack, look at the placement closely and guess which size will fit the best. If you guess on the first try, give yourself one point. Second try, no points; third try or more, negative one. Now set ten pieces. Depending on how intricate the placements are, try to get a score of at least five. If your score is near zero, keep working at it. If you consistently score below zero, you better stick to leading easy routes where you can hang around to fiddle with gear.

Take the same training to your routes. Avoid the tendency to always fire in a cam; instead, keep your mind open to passive protection opportunities. Focus on getting the right size piece on the first try.

CHAPTER 4

Mia Axon on Sphinx Crack (5.13), South Platte, Colorado

Cams

The ambiance of the desert, combined with the thousands of perfect cracks, makes Indian Creek, Utah, a dream to many climbers. In Indian Creek the cracks are parallel, and you need cams—lots of 'em. A single pitch often requires seven or more of the same size cam. This area has single-handedly funded the climbing cam companies.

Leaving the ground you feel the calm comfort of good jams; you climb high to the first cam, make another good run to the second, then you find a rhythm: jam, jam, jam, jam, set pro, start over.

The first climbers in Indian Creek didn't have any cams. It was the introduction of Friends in 1978 that really set climbers free in Indian Creek and other crack climbing

A complete set of cams covers cracks from less than a centimeter wide up to 16 centimeters (.4 to 6.5 inches). Usually the biggest cams stay at home; they come out only when wide cracks loom.

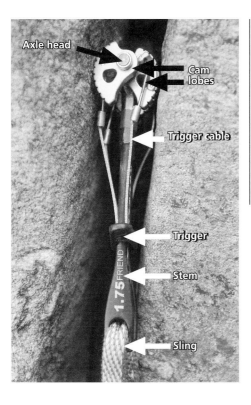

Axle head

Cam lobes

Trigger cable

Trigger

Stem

1.75 FRIEND

Sling

areas. Suddenly, parallel and irregular cracks became fast and easy to protect—no more fiddling around with chocks that would just rattle down the crack. Instead, fire the cam in, clip it, and go!

This chapter describes:
- the evolution of cams for climbing
- how cams work
- how to set and remove cams
- good and bad cam placements
- tips for freeing stuck cams

This Wild Country Technical Friend evolved from the original Friends. The basic design remains the same: two sets of opposing, spring-loaded cam lobes arranged on an axle, with a trigger for retracting the cam lobes when setting or removing the cam. The trigger rides along the flexible stem, making a handle for the climber. Most cams come with a sewn sling for clipping.

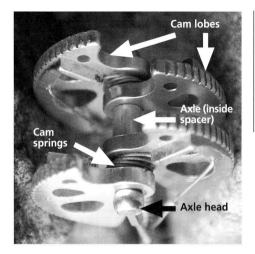

The chapter also discusses key aspects of cam design, including:

- cam lobes
- axles
- expansion range
- stem
- sling
- color coding

This DMM Four Cam Unit has a flexible U-shaped stem, an extendable sling, and light-weight cam lobes.

NUTS VERSUS CAMS

Often the crack dictates what type of gear to place. Cams work best in parallel cracks, while nuts and hexes work better in convoluted, wavy cracks. Sometimes you have lots of options for what to set, so you place nuts to save the cams for later.

Wired nuts are light and cheap, so you can carry a bundle of them, and it won't break your budget to leave a few to bail off a route. Nothing goes in fast like a cam though, a definite plus on hard pitches. A well-set cam also has the ability to swivel and withstand an outward or even upward pull, so cams are good at belays and as the first piece in a pitch. Cams also expand continuously through their expansion range, so they fit any size crack in that range, whereas a nut or hex only has two or three sizes.

CAM EVOLUTION

The idea of camming first entered the climbing world in 1958, when Swiss guide Adolf Jüsy and engineer Walter Marti introduced Jumar rope ascenders for climbing up ropes. Expanding on that idea, Greg Lowe created the Lowe Cam Nuts. They came to market in 1973, making them the first spring-loaded cams designed for anchoring. This design probably influenced Ray Jardine, who developed his Friends in secrecy during the mid-1970s, as he ticked many of Yosemite Valley's first 5.12 routes using his prototypes. He also climbed what was probably the first 5.13 in the world, *The Phoenix*. Friends were introduced to the climbing world in 1978, and they became the first commercially successful camming unit.

The cams that started it all: the original Wild Country Friends. These units are still usable (barely) twenty-five years later.

When the rigid-stemmed Wild Country Friends came onto the market, traditional rock climbing was changed forever. Overnight, parallel cracks that had been a nightmare to climb became easily protectable. Friends were initially available in only three sizes, 1 through 3. Soon a number 4 became available, and a couple years later four half-sizes were introduced (.5 to 3.5) to offer continuous coverage of cracks from 1.7 to 8.6 cm (0.67 to 3.4 inches). Today's Friends are available in 14 different sizes, offering a useful size range from a tiny 1.0 cm (0.4 inches) to the burly off-width size of 16 cm (6.5 inches).

Shortly after Friends became available, other inventors went to work tweaking the design. The cable U-stem pioneered by Steve Byrne and Doug Phillips allowed cams to be set in horizontal cracks without risk of breaking the stem, and their TCU (three cam unit) design enabled camming units to fit into shallow cracks. The German Stefan Engers introduced the single cable stem with his Jokers in 1985. This flexible stem worked well in many crack configurations, and Wild Country soon offered this style with their Technical Friends.

Dave Waggoner created the internal cam spring design of the Aliens in the mid-1980s. This design provides the strength and security of four cams, but allows the cams to fit closer on the axle for placement in shallow cracks. The internal cam spring also sets the cams more directly opposite of each other on the axle for improved performance in flared cracks. The same company also created Hybrid Aliens, with two different sizes of cams set on the axle to further accommodate flaring cracks and piton scars.

Inventor Tony Christianson developed the double-axle cam, which was introduced by Chouinard Equipment (later to become Black Diamond) in 1987. The double axle Camalots offered an increased expansion range, allowing a set of cams to cover a given size range with fewer pieces. This larger expansion range also made it easier to choose the right size of cam for a given placement. In 2005 the Camalots were re-introduced with 20 percent shaved off the weight. The following year, 2006, Black Diamond introduced the C-3, a futuristic three-cam design for thin cracks.

Doug Phillips added the Range Finder system to the Metolius TCUs and Power Cams (from #2 on up) in the early 2000s. This series of colored dots on the cam lobes helps climbers select the best unit for a given crack size. He also introduced Fat Cams for safer anchoring in soft rock and, in 2005, redesigned the TCUs and Power Cams to make them featherweight. Seth Murray and a team of three other University of Colorado students developed Splitter Cams, a design that opposes the cam lobes directly. This allows the unit to hold with only two cams contacting the rock in extremely shallow or flaring cracks (for aid climbing).

The TCU has only three cams so it fits small, shallow cracks.

Aliens have four closely-spaced cams, enabling them to fit small and shallow cracks. The crack opens above this placement. If leading, use a sling long enough to prevent rope wriggle from "walking" the cam.

Good expansion range and a secure feeling make the double-axle Camalot a favorite among climbers. The placement shown is terrible—the crack opens above and below. If the cam walks just a little it will fall out of the crack.

Metolius Power Cams are light and stable. The Range Finder system, a series of colored dots on the cam lobes, tells you when the cam fits the crack well. The Metolius cams also have a slightly different cam angle, which creates more horizontal force into the crack. This can help in marginal placements, but it costs some expansion range. This cam could be set a little deeper so the outer right cam isn't so close to the edge of the crack.

A. The inner two cams on the Metolius Supercam are smaller than the outer cams. The outer right cam is a bit too close to the edge of the crack in this placement.

B. The smaller cams can rotate an extra 180 degrees, allowing the unit to fit smaller cracks. This is not a good placement because the crack opens above—if the cam walks a little it won't work. A smaller size set lower and deeper in the crack would be better.

The Trango Max Cam uses three axles to seriously boost expansion range. The left, inner cam lobes ride on the middle axle, while the two outer cam lobes sit on axles attached to the opposing inner cam lobes; the axles retract with the cam lobes, allowing the units to fit smaller cracks. Like any cam, the Max Cam works better in the lower half of its expansion range; the cam lobes can become offset if the Max Cam walks. The Max Cam has an extendable clipping sling so you have three clipping lengths.

A. The Omega Pacific Link Cam offers three stages of emerging cams as you pull the trigger to produce a whopping 2:5 to 1 expansion range.

B. For a little extra weight and bulk, the Link Cams fit in an amazing range of cracks. They don't fit convoluted small cracks very well because of their bulk in the lower size ranges.

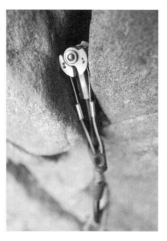

Left: The Trango Splitter Cam has directly opposing cam lobes. This allows the cams to fit shallow placements, and to work directly opposite each other for better performance in flared cracks. This cam is set too close to the crack's right edge.

The Wild Country Zero fits microcracks. The smallest two sizes are for aid, while the size shown (#3) and the next size will hold low-force leader falls—they break at 6 kN (1350 pounds). This placement could be set deeper for more security.

The Black Diamond C3 Camalot uses springs on the stem cables to drive the cams and has a protector for the trigger cables. The stem springs allow the cam lobes to be set closer together for fitting shallow placements. The smallest two sizes are strong enough for aid only.

The Metolius Fat Cams are designed for use in soft sandstone or other weak rock; their cam lobes are nearly twice as thick as most other cams. This large footprint decreases the pressure on the crack walls by spreading the load over more rock surface area, which makes the placement stronger.

This Wild Country hybrid Friend has #2 cams on the outside and #1.5 cams on the inside for fitting flared cracks. The placement shown is not good—it's too close to the edge of the crack on the right side and the outer left cam is barely touching the rock.

CAM PHYSICS

Just how does that camming unit hold a fall? The answer is friction. Due to the precisely calculated curve of the cam face, the lobes transfer downward force (created by a falling or hanging climber) into an outward force that's twice as great, directed against the crack walls. By pushing outward so hard, the camming unit creates friction between the cam faces and the crack walls to oppose the downward pull.

Due to the massive potential force on a cam, the rock surrounding the crack needs to be solid—a loose block or flake can easily get pried loose by a loaded camming unit. The rock surface where the cams touch also needs to be solid, not flaky, grainy, gritty, dirty, or lichen-coated. In poor rock the cams can pulverize the rock grains and pull out.

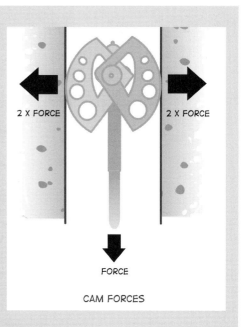

2 X FORCE

2 X FORCE

FORCE

CAM FORCES

Cams will hold even in a slightly flaring crack. The less "grippy" the rock is, the less flare angle a cam can endure. In very slippery rock a cam may not hold even in a parallel crack because there isn't enough friction.

SETTING AND REMOVING CAMS

When setting a cam, seek a uniformly parallel spot in the crack where the crack walls are parallel-sided, not wavering, ridged, bumpy, tapering, or flared. You can set a camming unit in non-parallel spots, and often must, but the best, most predictable placements exist in a parallel area of the crack.

If you don't have a parallel spot, set the cam above (and below, if possible) a constriction, in one of the openings, to "trap" the cam and prevent it from walking—such a placement can be very stable. Also avoid placements that rely on a small bump or bulge of rock that could break and cause the cam to pull out, or that allow the cam to easily walk. Don't set placements just above a flare or other openings because if the unit slips a little, it has no rock left to grip and it's outta there!

Cams are stable when they:

- open between 10 percent and 50 percent of full expansion
- open symmetrically
- contact solid rock

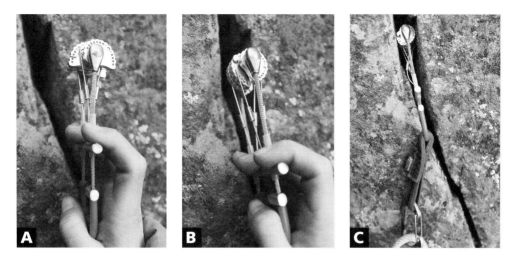

Setting a Cam

A. *Find a uniformly parallel spot in the crack where the rock is solid and clean. Choose the right size cam for the crack.*

B. *Pull the trigger to retract the cam lobes.*

C. *Insert the unit in the crack, release the trigger so the cams open to fit the crack, and orient the stem to point in the expected loading direction. Clip your rope into the cam. This is a good cam placement, with a lip just above the cam to prevent it from walking. The cam could be set slightly deeper to avoid blowing out the edge if the rock is soft at all.*

TO REMOVE A CAM

Pull the trigger bar to disengage the cams, then remove the piece from the crack. Look at the crack and imagine how the unit went in, then try to work it out through the same path, where the crack is widest. Usually the cam comes out easily, but sometimes the leader sets the unit too tight, or the cam walks to a tighter position. If the unit feels stuck pull the trigger harder to fully retract the cam lobes. You may need to slide the cam sideways out of the crack, or up or down, or wriggle it loose.

If the piece feels stuck, be patient—one hasty move might jam the piece tighter. You may need to hang from the rope or a piece of gear to free both hands for working on the cam. Sometimes, rather than hanging on the rope and blowing your free ascent, you can climb the rest of the pitch free, then lower back down to get the piece.

When you pull the trigger, try to identify which cam lobe is causing the unit to be stuck (in the worst case, all four cam lobes are jamming). Use your fingers on the cam lobe (or lobes) to help retract them. If the crack is too tight, a nut tool might help retract the individual cam lobes. Keep working the unit (assuming that you have time to waste on your climb); if the cam lobes can move at all, it's possible to get the cam out. If none of the cam lobes budges, give it up—the piece is fixed.

If you can't reach the trigger bar, take two wired nuts and slide the heads down on the cable (assuming that they are not fixed on the cable). Clip both nuts to a carabiner, and use the cable loops to snag each side of the trigger bar (this works better on some models of cams than others). Now pull the carabiner, while pushing on the stem or thumb loop, to retract the cam lobes.

On many routes you'll see fixed cam-ming units that someone couldn't remove. These make great booty if you can remove them. Inspect the liberated unit thoroughly before trusting it, and replace the sling.

GOOD AND BAD CAM PLACEMENTS

After you set a cam, check the cam lobes to make sure they all engage the rock so you have a stable placement. If the placement is not great, retract the trigger and find a more stable spot. Some of the ways to avoid setting your cams are shown in the following pictures.

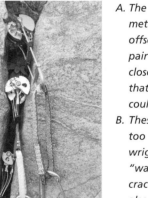

This is a bomber cam place-ment. The cam lobes are open slightly less than halfway, in a solid, parallel section of the crack.

A. The cams should be sym-metrically deployed, not offset as these are. If one pair of cams that's nearly closed opposes another set that's nearly open, the unit could fail.

B. These cams are open too wide, so a little rope wriggle can make the unit "walk" deeper into the crack. The outer cams are also open wider than the inner cams, which makes the unit less stable.

C. If you force a camming unit into a tight spot its cams may jam. When fully com-pressed the cams can't get any smaller for removal, so they can become hopelessly stuck in the crack.

The crack opens up right below this cam, so if it slips just a
little it's toast.

Moving the same cam slightly
higher to a more parallel spot
in the crack greatly enhances
its security.

This rigid-stemmed cam might
break on the rock edge if it
takes a hard load. The placement would be better if it
were set deeper in the crack to
reduce leverage on the stem.

A camming unit set in a horizontal crack. A hard fall might kink the cables, but a well-placed unit will still hold the fall. Horizontal placements are somewhat less predictable than vertical ones, however.

The tie-off high on the stem of this Friend prevents loading the rigid stem over an edge. Unlike a cable stem, it won't get kinked from repeated loading in horizontal cracks.

This crack is quite flaring—the cam may or may not hold in a quick loading. Because the rock has good friction, the placement seems okay, but a less flared placement would be better.

This cam is horrendously unstable. A little rope wriggle will walk it right out of its placement.

A cam generates twice as much outward force as the downward load it holds, so in a fall it can easily pry off a block or flake. The falling rock could injure you, your partner, your rope, or all three.

CAM TESTING

In 1994 I conducted a number of strength tests on cams set in good granite and soft sandstone. These tests were conducted with a slow-pull machine, which is more severe than the fast loading and unloading in a real fall. In most tests the units failed at loads between 12.5 and 14 kN (2800 to 3100 pounds)—plenty strong enough to hold most real-life falls. The strongest cam managed to hold around 19 kN (4250 pounds) before it exploded through the soft sandstone rock; at this point the axle was severely deformed.

The weakest cam, however, held about 0.5 kN (115 pounds) before it broke a thin sandstone flake. Other cams failed at frighteningly low loads near or below 4 kN (900 pounds), if: the cam lobes were open too wide; the piece was set in a flare in soft sandstone; the piece was set near the edge of the crack in soft sandstone; or if the piece was set behind a loose block. A smart climber avoids placements like these.

In the soft sandstone many of the cams punched through the harder surface layer at around 7 kN (1600 pounds). Once this happened the cams would continue pulverizing the surface layer and slide out of the crack. When leading on soft sandstone you're wise to set the cams fairly close together to minimize the length of a fall and the force created, and to have ample backup below in case a piece does fail. Belay anchors should be well-equalized as well. Another way to increase anchor strength in soft sandstone is to use Metolius Fat Cams, which have cam lobes that are much thicker than most other units. These spread the load over a wider surface area of rock, which decreases the pressure on the crack walls.

CAM DESIGN

Any cam design is a balancing act: weight against strength, "holding power" against expansion range, durability against cost. To choose the best cams, decide how you will use them and what features are most useful. Don't base your decision solely on dollars; it's better to choose the cams that provide the most security and utility for the lightest weight.

Cam Lobes. Cam lobes are the heart of a cam. The lobes' curvature is designed to create the same cam interception angle (the angle between a line drawn from the axle to where the cam contacts the rock, and a line perpendicular to the crack wall—see drawing next page) throughout a cam's expansion range. A smaller cam angle creates greater outward force on the crack wall, which increases its chances of holding in a flare, slick rock, or other irregular placement. Increasing the cam angle adds expansion range, but if the cam angle is too greedy, the unit won't create enough friction to hold.

Most of the cam companies have settled on a cam angle around 13.75 degrees.

When pull-tested in a lab, cams are generally set in a perfect parallel placement in a testing jig, with the stem aligned exactly along the direction of pull. A force is applied and progressively increased until the unit fails. While the constant force

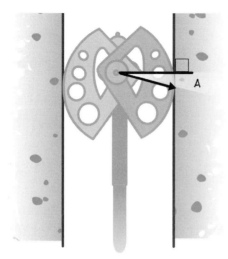

A= CAM INTERCEPTION ANGLE

The curvature of the cam lobes determines their interception angle with the rock.

during a pull test can be harsher than the split-second loading of an actual leader fall, in real rock the placements are often not perfect. The crack may be flared, or the stem may not align with the direction of pull, which can create higher stress on the cams. For this reason, some companies "overbuild" their cams, making them stronger than they need to be for the perfect pull in a testing lab. On the other extreme, cams with large cutouts in the cam lobes may be light, but they may crumple during a bad fall. The UIAA requires only 5 kN (1125 pounds) in a strength test to certify cams, which is well below worst-case loading in a leader fall.

Most camming units have four cam lobes, which spreads the load over two contact points on each side of the crack. Four cams offer stability in most placements, but if the rope wriggles the piece, the four cams can "walk" inside the crack. When the stem gets rotated up, the outer two cams walk deeper into the crack; when the stem rotates down the inner two cams walk. If the unit gets rotated back-and-forth it can walk progressively deeper into the crack. When this happens the cams can become so tight that they get stuck, the trigger can bury itself beyond reach, or the cam lobes can open and become unstable. Set a long sling on cams that you suspect might walk to prevent the rope from wriggling them when leading.

Some companies offer three-cam units (commonly known as TCUs) in the smaller sizes: a single cam on one side of the axle opposes two cams on the other side. With only three cams taking up space on the axle, TCUs can squeeze into shallow cracks. Three-cam units are also less prone to walking than four-cam models. The middle cam lobe does concentrate the pressure on one side of the crack wall, so the companies make the middle cam lobe significantly thicker than the two opposing cams to distribute force and partially alleviate this problem.

Some companies mill grooves into the cam lobes' contact surface (where the cam meets the rock). The grooves do not help the actual camming performance, but they can grip small crystals or texture on the rock surface to add stability to the placement. They also may allow a space for broken tiny rock fragments to settle in a hard pull, so the cam lobe can still contact solid rock.

The thickness of the cam lobes' contact face determines how much pressure they will exert where the cam lobes meet the crack wall. A thicker cam lobe decreases pressure on the rock by spreading the load over more rock surface, reducing the chance of rock failure. A thicker cam lobe also weighs more. Most models of cams have lobes that are about 6-millimeters (.25-inches) thick.

Early models of cams had cam lobes that could invert in a hard pull if the cams were open too wide—both cams would flop over the axle like a blown-out umbrella. Most modern cams have some sort of stop that prevents the cams from inverting, which creates a little more security when the cam is set at its absolute widest range, or when placed chock-style in a constriction. Some cam stops also add thickness to the cams when they're near full retraction, so you get more surface contact with the rock in the cam's smaller size range.

Axles. Most camming units have cam lobes mounted on a single axle. Black Diamond's patented Camalot double-axle was the first design to increase expansion range, at the cost of a higher weight. Trango's triple-axle design further increases expansion range, with only a slight penalty in weight.

Stem. Rigid-stemmed Friends are more durable than cams with flexible stems, and they load more predictably, but they should not be set with the stem protruding over the edge of a horizontal or diagonal crack.

Most cams these days have flexible stems, which bend to reduce leverage when loaded in a horizontal placement. A single

EXPANSION RANGE

Some of the newest cams offer unprecedented expansion range, so a unit fits in a wider range of crack sizes. Greater expansion makes it easier to choose the right size for the crack; it also improves a cam's performance in flares because the back cams can be closed tight while the front cams are still open pretty wide (like a hybrid cam). The big expansion range allows you to carry fewer cams on some routes, but on a rope-stretching pitch that eats 20 cams, lighter units will give you a fighting chance.

Most companies list a cam's absolute expansion in their promotional literature (cam lobes fully retracted to fully open), which is misleading. Ideally the cam lobes should sit between about 10 percent and 50 percent expanded; in a pinch you can squeak out a slightly larger placement, or squeeze the cam tighter. Set a cam fully retracted, though, and your partner is likely to spend an hour trying to retrieve it—or worse, leave it fixed in the crack. Leave the lobes open too wide, in the cam's larger expansion range, and the cam will be unstable and may walk or pull out in a fall.

EXPANSION RANGE CHART

Standard cams	1:1.5
Double axle cams	1:1.6 – 1:1.7
Supercam	1:1.8
Max Cam	1:2.0
Link Cam	1:2.5

This chart shows the ratio from cams fully retracted to cams fully open for the various cam designs. The true, "safe" expansion ratio is somewhat less than shown, because cams should always be placed at less than full expansion.

cable stem will also bend in a vertical placement if the stem is not aligned with the direction of pull. The single stem attaches in the middle of the axle, so it spreads the cam lobes wider on the axle to give more stability. A single stem can slightly reduce a cam's tendency to walk because the stem's flexibility absorbs wriggle from the rope. Adding a longer sling to the placement, however, works better.

Some models of cams have a U-stem, which bends well when the cam is placed in a horizontal orientation, but not in a vertical alignment. U-stem units can be more prone to walking when set in a vertical crack, but can realign as a fall's force comes onto the cam. The U-stem also protects the trigger cables from wear and kinking, provides rigidity when you're stretching for a far-away placement, and furnishes a high clip-in point for aid climbing. The U-stem also allows the cam lobes to sit closer on the axle, enabling them to fit narrow placements. In bigger sizes, though, close cam lobes are less stable; most climbers find the U-stem most beneficial in the smaller sizes.

Trigger Bar and Thumb Catch. Climbing already exacts enough of a toll on our fingers—we don't need our cams adding to the misery. Fortunately, most cams have a fairly ergonomic and digit-friendly trigger design. A stem loop surrounding the thumb catch decreases the chance that you'll drop the cam (especially when wearing gloves for alpine climbing), and allows a place for short-clipping when you're aid climb-

COLOR CODING

In a perfect world climbing companies would standardize the color-coding system so that you could easily identify a cam's size no matter what brand you were using. Currently Black Diamond, DMM, Omega Pacific, Trango, and Wild Country share colors for similar size cams (though not a similar numbering system); other companies are all over the map.

With practice you'll learn the color-coding system and eventually relate a certain color to the type of jam you get in the crack (for example, good finger jams means silver #1 Friend, good hand jam means gold #2 Camalot, etc.). With even more experience you'll be able to simply look at the crack and pick the right size of cam.

A. Cams with an extendable sling provide three clipping points: you can clip directly to the stem for maximum reach in aid climbing.

B. Clip to the doubled sling to minimize extension in straight-up cracks.

C. Or clip to the extended sling to reduce rope drag and minimize rope wriggle on the cam.

ing. Textured grips make it easier to hang onto a unit when you're pumped, or when the air oozes with humidity. Try triggering each size of a model of cams before buying to make sure the trigger system fits your hand—some designs are not great for climbers with small hands.

Sling. Some companies use strong, durable, and highly cut-resistant Spectra webbing (called Dyneema on the European cams). The extra strength afforded by this high-tech material allows for a lighter, thinner sling to be used, but at an additional expense over nylon. Nylon slings are more susceptible to snagging and wear, but less costly.

Many models of cams have a versatile, extendable sling so you can clip close to the cam to minimize your fall length, or extend the sling to reduce rope drag. This adds a little extra weight and bulk to the cam, but allows you to carry fewer quickdraws.

Offset Cams. A couple of companies offer camming units with two different sizes of cams mounted on the axle. You can set the smaller cam lobes deep in the crack, while the larger cam lobes sit on the outside, for a good fit in a flared crack. These are somewhat specialized, but they work great in flared cracks and piton scars, and are especially useful for aid climbing.

Giant Cams. Giant camming units protect offwidth cracks. They're heavy and cumbersome, but you can slide them up a nasty gash to maintain overhead protection as you lead, and they work well in mildly flared wide cracks. Sling the unit with a quickdraw or long sling when leading above the cam, because giant cams easily walk and tip into a sketchy position if the rope wriggles them. You'll only want to carry these unwieldy things when you know you'll need them.

Andy Johnson pushing his big cam up Big Pink *(5.11), Vedauwoo, Wyoming*

Big cams can become unstable and flop over, especially when set in their larger size range or when set at the lip of a roof like this cam on Lucille *(5.12).*

EXERCISE—CAM SCHOOL

New Trad Climber:

Round up all the cams you can, at least a full set, and head to a cliff that has cracks at the base (and no climbers above). Practice placing the different sizes of cams, and if possible get a guide or experienced climber to check your placements. Yank the sling downward, and pull it up to see if the cam rotates to hold the new pull. Practice setting many cams; look closely at the crack width and try to correctly choose which size cam to set on the first try.

Intermediate Trad Climber:

Take a bunch of cams to the cliff base and set ten of them as fast as you can. You get one point if you pick the right size on the first try, no points for the second try, and minus one for three or more tries. A score above five means that you have a decent eye for setting cams, but you can still get better. A score near zero means keep practicing.

CHAPTER 5

Anna McConica top-roping at Horsetooth Reservoir, Colorado

Top-rope and Rappel Anchors

Devils Lake, Wisconsin, is made up of bullet-hard quartzite. The cliffs aren't super tall, and most routes don't offer much lead protection, so most climbers top-rope. This is a great way to start climbing or to push your limits, because falling is usually safe.

Top-roping can also be a fun way for larger groups to climb together, which is common at Devils Lake. True to friendly midwestern values, people even invite you onto their top rope as you hike the cliff line. On most climbs you'll top out, see good anchors and rigging, and lower back off. Once in awhile, though, you'll find anchors frightful enough that you decline to lower and walk back down instead. If that happens to you, politely recommend this book to the anchor-builder and find another rope to climb on.

This chapter covers what you need to know for building top-rope anchors using natural anchors or chocks and cams. It covers how to:

- rig a slingshot top rope, with the anchors on top of the cliff and the belayer on the ground below
- set a top rope with the belayer on top of the cliff
- protect yourself when setting anchors near the cliff's edge
- haul your partner if they can't get up the climb
- evaluate fixed rappel anchors
- clean up messy anchors

In a top-rope fall or bouncy rappel the force on the anchors can be several times body weight, but they are not subjected to the huge forces of a leader fall unless your team makes a big mistake. Still, on every rappel and top rope you trust your life to the system, so it's crucial to have good anchors for safety.

Once you complete a top-rope climb, you can walk off, lower down, or rappel, depending on the situation.

TOP-ROPE RACK

You don't need much gear to top-rope. If you're on a budget, forego the expensive camming units and buy hexagonal chocks and wired nuts instead. If you do buy cams for top-roping only, the cheaper models will work fine because you don't need the same performance that you want for lead climbing. A general rack for top-roping may include the following:

- 1 set of wired nuts
- 1 set of cams or slung chocks ranging from 3/4 to 3 inches
- 1 40- to 60-foot-long piece of 1-inch tubular webbing or 10-millimeter diameter or bigger climbing rope (static rope works best)
- 6 shoulder-length slings
- 2 double-length slings
- 4-6 carabiners
- 2-4 locking carabiners
- 1 7- or 8-millimeter diameter cordelette, 6 meters (20 feet) long
- 1 nut tool

Tailor your equipment list to meet the requirements of the area. Some top-roping areas may require different gear than what's listed above. For example, if the top anchors are bolted, you will need only a fraction of the gear listed above. Do your research before heading out.

Rack for rigging two bolted top-rope stations:

- 4 carabiners
- 4 locking carabiners
- 2 double-length slings or 4 shoulder slings
- Extra slings in case the bolts are not close together.
- Backup material if the bolts are not bomber

SLINGSHOT TOP ROPE

Probably the most common way that climbers top-rope is by using a slingshot setup: the belayer is on the ground and the rope runs up to the top anchors, then back down to the climber. This allows good visibility and communication between the belayer and the climber, and it puts the belayer in a good position to hold the climber's weight: the carabiners at the top anchor create enough friction that the belayer feels only about 60 percent of the climber's weight, and the belayer is getting pulled up rather than down, so she can use her body weight to counterbalance the climber.

A ground anchor is generally not required when slingshot top-roping because of the friction at the top anchor. If the climber greatly outweighs the belayer, however, the belayer should be anchored to the ground. The belayer should also be anchored if she is positioned far from the spot that is directly below the anchors, to keep her from getting dragged along the ground when the climber weights the rope.

If the team has constructed solid anchors and is using good belaying techniques, the biggest potential hazard probably involves rockfall. For this reason, the belayer should not be positioned directly below the climber, and especially should not be anchored beneath the climber.

ANCHORS AT THE CLIFF EDGE

When rigging a top rope, extend the anchors over the lip of the cliff so that the rope runs straight up, through the master point carabiners, and straight back down. If the anchors are not extended and sit above the edge, the rope must bend over the cliff edge, pass through the carabiners, and bend back over the cliff edge. This creates serious rope drag and the rope may get damaged if the cliff edge is even a little sharp.

It's convenient to set anchors near the edge of the cliff when possible to minimize the distance that you need to extend them. Some areas are equipped with bolts for building top-rope anchors, which makes rigging easy. Other times you may find cracks or other anchor possibilities at the edge of the cliff. Either way, two good bolts, or three solid anchors, rigged to ERNEST standards, will make a good top-rope anchor. Sometimes a huge tree or giant boulder may be used as the sole anchor; the team needs to make a good judgment call on whether this is adequate.

The standard equalized and pre-equalized riggings shown in chapter 1 will work great if you have two good bolts or three natural anchors close together. For more options see the belay anchor arrangements rigged with slings or a cordelette in chapter 7, Traditional Belay Anchors; these can easily be adapted to top-roping by omitting the upward direction anchor (if one exists) and extending the anchor over the cliff edge.

PROTECTING YOURSELF WHILE RIGGING

It can be dangerous setting anchors at the edge of the cliff—one slip and it's all over. To safeguard this process, build a good anchor back from the edge of the cliff and fix a rope to this anchor. Use the fixed rope to protect yourself while you rig the top-rope anchor. Attach to the fixed rope with a Prusik or clove hitch so you can easily adjust the extension to keep yourself tight to the anchors.

Prusik

The clove hitch is a bomber way to attach to the fixed rope, and it is only slightly less convenient to adjust than the Prusik.

A Prusik attached to a fixed line allows you to safely rig anchors at the edge of the cliff. It's wise to also tie into the fixed rope to back up the Prusik.

TWO-BOLT TOP-ROPE ANCHOR

If you have bolts, you can quickly set up a pre-equalized anchor for top-roping.

Two shoulder-length slings rigged with the sliding X makes a redundant anchor with no supertight knots to untie when you're done.

ANCHORS EXTENDED OVER THE EDGE

Often you can't find good anchors at the cliff edge, or it may be an inconvenient place to rig. In these cases you can set the anchors back from the edge and extend them to drop the master point over the lip. Always use at least two separate sets of sling, cord, or rope to extend over the lip, for redundancy, and pad any sharp edges with a small patch of carpet, a pack, or even a t-shirt (don't use your favorite t-shirt though).

TOP BELAY

Acadia National Park has some beautiful, popular sea cliffs that are climbed mostly

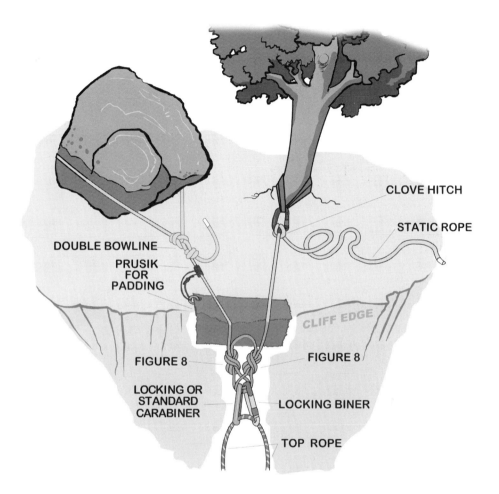

CLOVE HITCH

STATIC ROPE

DOUBLE BOWLINE

PRUSIK FOR PADDING

CLIFF EDGE

FIGURE 8

FIGURE 8

LOCKING OR STANDARD CARABINER

LOCKING BINER

TOP ROPE

Many options exist for extending the anchors past the cliff edge. This method uses a piece of 10 millimeter-diameter static rope. The rigging rope is tied around a large boulder with a double bowline and extended over the lip, where a master point is created by tying a figure eight on a bight. A second master point is tied right next to the first one for redundancy; then the rope runs back to the second anchor, a large tree, which is fixed with a sling. The rigging rope is tied to the sling with a clove hitch, and the clove hitch is adjusted so both anchors help hold the load. Finally, an old patch of carpet pads the edge, and is held in place by a Prusik attached to the rigging rope.

on top rope. The belayer anchors on top of the cliff, and the climber rappels or lowers down to a ledge just above the waterline, then gets a top rope as she climbs back out. The ambiance of the ocean and the seabirds makes the climbing seem even better than it is.

In a place like Acadia, where the bottom of the cliff is inaccessible but it's easy to get to the top, it makes sense to belay from the top. A top belay also might be used if rockfall makes belaying from the ground dangerous, or if the team is only climbing on the last pitch of a tall cliff. It can also come in handy if the cliff is taller than half a rope length, and the team only has one rope (a better option may be to tie two ropes together and use the slingshot system). The top belay may put all of the climber's weight on the belayer and may make communication difficult, so the slingshot system is usually preferable.

With a top belay, the climber is often lowered down the cliff, and then climbs back up. If lowering will possibly damage the rope, or if it might be difficult for the climber to communicate when it's time to stop being lowered, the climber can also rappel, then be belayed back up on the rappel line, if a good ledge or anchors exist for the transition from rappelling to climbing. An even safer option is to rappel on one rope while being belayed on another, then to climb with protection from the belay rope. Logistics must be well-planned and communicated between the climbers to avoid problems.

A. When lowering a climber it's easiest (and possibly safest) to lower directly off the anchors. A great system for the direct lower is to use a standard belay device attached to the anchors as shown. Redirect the rope through a high carabiner (attached to the "top shelf" here) to create the necessary bend across the belay device and to add friction.

Belayer clip-in

End of the rope

Autoblock

to climber

B

Belaying off the harness can work, but if the climber weights the rope it may be uncomfortable for the belayer, especially if the climber hangs for an extended time.

B. For more control, add a friction hitch such as the autoblock shown here (see appendix 2 for how to tie the autoblock). The autoblock is especially important if the belayer is at risk of rockfall, lightning, or some other hazard. Here the end of the rope is tied off so you can't lower the end of the rope through the device, and the belayer is anchored into the top shelf with a sling.

Belaying directly off the anchors with a self-locking belay device like a Petzl GriGri or Trango Cinch makes it easy to hold a fall. It may be a little jerky to lower this way, so you can lower with the redirected system shown above, then belay with the self-locking device as shown. You need to understand the manufacturer's instructions for using these devices, and make sure that the locking cam is free to move (not jammed against the wall) so it can arrest the rope.

ADVANCED TIP—HAULING WITH A GRIGRI

When using a self-locking belay device you can easily create a Z-pulley system to haul your partner's sorry bones up the route if he cannot climb it. Theoretically the Z-pulley creates a 3:1 mechanical advantage, though with friction it might be more like 2:1 when using a GriGri or Cinch for the pulley.

Prusik

Set a Prusik or other friction hitch on the rope going down to the climber, and clip the brake strand to this friction hitch. Configure the rope to make a "Z" (the Z-pulley system), and pull on the brake strand. Once the friction hitch touches the belay device, slide it back down the rope and haul again.

RAPPEL ANCHORS

So you've topped out on *Time Wave Zero* (5.12b or 5.10 A1) in El Potrero Chico, Mexico. Now it's time to get down, via the twenty-three rappels. Fortunately the anchors are well bolted, with spare bolts for clipping the team comfortably into each rappel station. Having a good system for efficient rappelling will save hours on such a descent.

On any established rappel descent, rappel anchors are fixed in place. The anchors serve two purposes: the climbing team clips them for protection when they arrive at the station, and then they use them to anchor their rappel rope(s) for the next rappel.

Fortunately, beefy, well-designed rappel stations are becoming prevalent, although you can still find plenty of chossy old rappel anchors. It's up to the climbing team to decide if the anchors and rigging are adequate, and to rebuild or rerig them if necessary. All climbers have a stake in the condition of anchors, so we also have a duty to replace or improve poor anchor setups. Some of the tattered rappel stations that still exist (usually in alpine or low-use areas) are pretty low-rent, and could definitely use a makeover. Sacrificing some time and gear beats risking your life on sketchy rappel anchors, and it helps prevent the horrifying "I-wonder-if-the-anchors-are-gonna-hold?" rappels.

BOLTED RAPPEL ANCHORS

Two or more good bolts in solid rock make a strong, convenient anchor for rappelling. The bolts also need to be fixed with rings or links for passing the rope through. Older stations may have webbing or cord fixing the rappel ring(s) to the anchors. This is okay if the material is relatively new and in good condition, but it looks trashy, and the nylon material breaks down with exposure to the elements and ultraviolet radiation. A much better setup has rings fixed directly to the bolt hangers, with no webbing or cord involved.

These commercially available Fixe rings make great hardware for clipping, lowering, and rappelling. The round rings are free to turn so wear is not concentrated in a single point, which increases their useful life.

Some climbers might worry that this arrangement only has one ring, but since the welded steel ring is stronger than the climbing rope, it's perfectly acceptable (provided that the weld was done correctly).

In high-use areas it's nice if the lowering/rappelling hardware is easy to replace. One convenient system is to combine an 8-millimeter ($^5/_{16}$-inch) diameter rapid link with an 8-millimeter ($^5/_{16}$-inch) diameter lap link; once the lap link starts to wear thin, just unscrew the rapid link and replace it. This can be done quickly and cheaply. The arrangement shown would be better still if the bolts were set at the same level.

8–10 millimeter ($^5/_{16}$–$^3/_8$ inch) diameter steel chain works nicely for feeding a rope through. Ideally the climbers who installed the hardware painted the chain (and bolts) camouflage, and they cut the chain sections short so that they are not an eyesore. It's not ideal if the bolts are fixed directly through the chain links because this causes unnecessary leverage on the bolts. It's better if the chain is attached to a bolt hanger, as shown.

Left: The opening of the rings should be perpendicular to the rock, as in all the examples above. If the openings face the rock, (as they would here if the rope were not twisting them toward a perpendicular orientation), lowering a climber or pulling a rappel rope down can seriously twist the rope.

PITON, CHOCK, AND NATURAL RAPPEL ANCHORS

A stout, living, well-rooted tree can make a strong, convenient rappel anchor. Simply tie two wraps of webbing around the tree, ideally fixed with two rapid links or rappel rings. If the tree is burly enough, you can fix the slings above a branch for a convenient, high location. Smaller trees should be slung near the ground where the sling creates less leverage.

A solid, large rock tunnel fixed with slings and rappel rings makes a good, easy-to-rig rappel anchor.

When rappelling off a rock horn, make sure the horn has a good positive lip for holding the slings, and be careful to load the anchor in a downward direction when beginning the rappel. This rock horn doesn't look very secure; I'd rather find another way down.

Left: If the horn was good, you could quickly add two extra pieces of cord to back up the single sling and the rappel ring. It's good to carry a small knife and some cord or webbing for such operations.

131

A rurp, a copperhead, and a piton rigged with tattered cord, faded webbing, and a single aluminum rappel ring. Don't settle for bad rappel anchors like these.

A couple pieces of fresh cord, a steel rapid link, and a couple of nuts turned the nightmare anchor into something reasonable. A piece of cord ties into both nuts and is pre-equalized, with overhand knots. Another sling is girth-hitched to the master point and pre-equalized with the piton. The old aluminum ring and a steel rapid link rappel rings are attached to the new master point, and the old sling backs up the cord.

If you want to ensure that the load is perfectly equalized between the nuts and the piton, create an equalizer. All the knots shown are overhands except the water knot left of the piton (use a triple fisherman's instead of a water knot if your cord manufacturer calls for it). This rigging gives half the load to the piton, while the other half is split by the nuts. The extension-limiting knots are tied close to minimize extension if one side fails.

  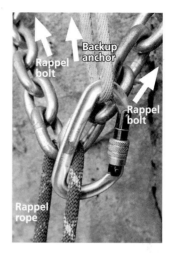

This anchor is bad all around. It depends on a single flake, and it's rigged in the old-school American Triangle, which amplifies forces on the pieces. The V-angle in the sling is close to 90 degrees, the sling is tied in a fashion that eliminates redundancy, and the rope runs directly through the cord. Not much to recommend here.

You can dress it up but you still can't take it out. The anchor still relies solely on one flake.

You can set extra pieces to back up the rappel anchors, to be cleaned by the last person down. In theory that should be the lightest climber because she is least likely to make the anchors fail. It's no fun always being the one without a backup anchor, though, so light climbers might protest this rule. Anyway, if the rappel anchors are sketchy, leave the backup in for the last person too. The gear will be sacrificed for a good cause, because the consequence of rappel anchor failure is usually death.

RAPPEL RINGS

Metal rappel rings create a low friction path for the rope to run through when pulling for retrieval, and they cannot be melted like a sling by having a rope pulled through. .

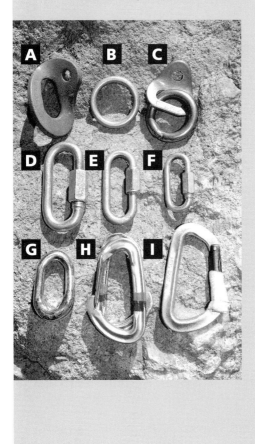

A. Bomber. The Metolius Enviro Rap Hanger makes a bomber attachment for anchoring or rappelling; a standard bolt hanger is not a safe rappel ring.

B. Okay. The ¼-inch (6mm) diameter aluminum rings are intended for one-time use in mountaineering settings. It's wise to check these for wear and to back them up.

C. Bomber. The Fixe hanger/ring combo with a ³/₈-inch (10 mm) diameter welded steel ring.

D. Bomber. A ³/₈-inch (10 mm) diameter Rapid Link can be opened for bolt maintenance.

E. Good. A ⁵/₁₆-inch (8 mm) diameter Rapid Link also makes a good removable link or rappel ring, and it's lighter than the ³/₈-inch model. Some climbers routinely carry a couple of these for re-rigging rappels.

F. Okay. The ¼-inch (6 mm) diameter Rapid Link is okay for one-time use but not great for permanent fixed hardware.

G. Bomber. A ³/₈-inch (10 mm) diameter lap link makes a cheap, strong rappel ring.

H. Bomber. You can always leave a locking carabiner as a rappel ring, or two carabiners with gates opposed as shown here.

I. Okay. In a pinch you can use a regular carabiner with the gate taped shut as a rappel ring.

EXERCISE—TOP-ROPE SCHOOL

The exercise is to spend a day top-rope climbing, and to practice different methods for rigging and belaying the top rope. Set up and climb on the following systems:

- a slingshot top rope with natural anchors
- a slingshot top rope with cams and chocks
- a top rope with the belayer on top of the cliff
- practice using a self-protection system while setting anchors near the cliff edge

CHAPTER 6

Cameron Cross climbing Have a Cigar *(5.12), Vinales, Cuba*

Sport Climbing Anchors

Smith Rock, Oregon lies in a beautiful gorge cut by the Crooked River. During the birth of sport climbing in America during the mid-to-late 1980s, the highly-featured volcanic rock was bolted to create a wealth of cutting edge sport routes. Many of the country's first 5.13 and 5.14 routes were climbed here, partly because Smith Rock was one of the first places where bolts proliferated.

Not all the routes are hard at Smith. You can find 5.7s a few dozen feet from 5.14s, with an abundance of everything in between. Some of the early bolted routes are spicy—the bolts are spaced a little further than on most modern sport routes. Generally, though, it's like any sport climbing area: with pre-placed bolts and little gear to carry, you can focus on the climbing. Because of the soft rock, some of the bolts are glue-ins, while others are standard mechanical bolts.

You welcome the sunshine that warms the rock as you check your knot and harness, the belayer's harness and belay device, and the stopper knot in the end of the rope. You make sure that you have enough quickdraws, all clipped in the same direction, with the rope-carabiner (the one fixed in the quickdraw, often with a bent gate) hanging on the bottom. You also carry a couple slings and extra carabiners for attaching yourself to the top anchors so you can rig the rope to lower at the top. Once you're certain that everything is in line, you start up the pitch, enjoying the feel of the rock on your fingertips.

The task of setting anchors and protection is simplified when sport climbing because the bolted anchors are already in place, waiting to be clipped.

This chapter tells you what to carry and gives a few considerations for clipping bolts, such as how to:
- align the quickdraws
- avoid dangerous carabiner orientations
- rig anchors for lowering and top-roping
- set up bolted belay stations for multi-pitch routes

SPORT CLIMBING RACK

For single-pitch sport routes you need only enough quickdraws to clip all the bolts, plus two for the top anchors, and one or two spares in case you drop one. Many climbers add a couple slings with locking carabiners for the transition from climbing to lowering. A typical sport climbing rack might include:

- 10-15 quickdraws
- 2 shoulder-length slings
- 2-3 extra carabiners
- 2-3 locking carabiners
- 1 belay device

You'll need some extra gear for arranging the belay anchors on multipitch sport routes. Add the following:

- 2 double-length slings for rigging belay stations
- 2 standard carabiners
- 4 locking carabiners
- 2 belay/rappel devices with locking carabiners

If the belay stations have more than two bolts, or if you plan to set gear to back up the belays, substitute a cordelette for the double slings. It's also a good idea to carry a small knife on multipitch routes in case you have a stuck rope or need to cut cord.

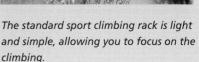

The standard sport climbing rack is light and simple, allowing you to focus on the climbing.

CLIPPING BOLTS

Ideally, the rope runs as straight as possible as you lead a route, because each bend in the rope adds drag. If the bolts lie in a fairly straight line, short quickdraws work fine. If the bolts wander, or the route climbs overhanging rock, longer quickdraws help the rope run clean. If a bolt is way off to the side, or far under a roof, a shoulder-length sling might provide enough extension to keep the rope running straight.

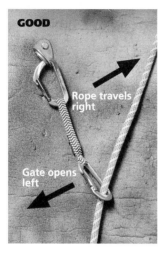

If the pitch traverses above the bolt, face the quickdraw so both gates open away from the direction of travel.

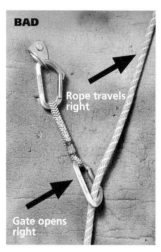

If the carabiner gate faces the direction of travel, it has a greater chance of unclipping during a fall.

Avoid backclipping the quickdraw, with the rope passing through the quickdraw toward the rock.

Backclipping increases the chance that the rope will accidentally unclip if you fall.

This quickdraw should be extended with a longer sling. As it is, the lip of the roof will cause lots of rope drag, and if the climber falls with protection above the roof, the rope will be loaded over the lip and possibly damaged.

Adding an extra quickdraw helps the rope run cleaner here.

DANGEROUS CARABINER ORIENTATIONS

Carabiners are strongest when loaded along their spine with the gate closed. If the gate gets pushed open, or if the carabiner gets cross-loaded or bent over an edge, the carabiner can lose enough strength to break in a hard fall. Pay attention to avoid dangerous carabiner orientations.

A carabiner loaded over an edge could break in a hard leader fall. A longer quickdraw would avoid this problem.

Avoid any orientation that allows the rock to push the carabiner gate open. If the gate opens during a fall, the carabiner can lose around two-thirds or more of its strength. Carabiners are marked with their full strength, gate-open strength, and cross-loaded strength. For safety, it's wise to buy carabiners that have high gate-open strength (9 or 10 kN/ 2025 or 2250 pounds).

This cross-loaded carabiner is sacrificing much of its strength. Pay special attention to make sure that carabiners get loaded along their spine.

A quickdraw with locking carabiners on both ends makes it impossible for the rope to accidentally unclip from critical bolts. This isn't a bad idea when accidental unclipping will result in injury, for example, when clipping the first bolts of a climb or when climbing above a ledge.

You can also use two quickdraws on a bolt, if the hanger is big enough. Clip the longer quickdraw on the outside of the hanger (farthest from the rock), so it does not get loaded unless a malfunction occurs with the quickdraw that lies closest to the rock. This technique would only be used when the climbing is hard and you're relying heavily on a single bolt.

RIGGING TOP ANCHORS FOR LOWERING AND TOP-ROPING

At busy climbing areas it's often best to lower back to the ground through your own carabiners to save wear on the fixed rings. The last climber down, however, often lowers from the fixed hardware. The rope should pass through steel rings or chain links attached to at least two bolts. Most bolt hangers are sharp on the inside, and they are not intended for passing the rope directly through. Metolius rap hangers are the exception. Sometimes the last climber down rappels rather than lowering, to save wear on the fixed rings and the rope. Before the climber begins climbing, the climber and belayer should discuss whether the climber is going to lower or rappel from the top.

This is a standard setup for lowering back to the ground. Utilizing one quickdraw per bolt, face the carabiner gates out so the carabiners don't interfere with each other's gates.

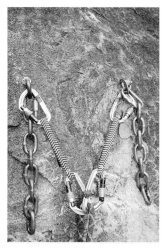

It's okay to top-rope through two standard quickdraws, but if one or both of them is fixed with locking carabiners it's even more bomber.

You can't be mindless about your anchors, even when sport climbing. The leader down-climbed this pitch rather than being lowered from these rusty seaside bolts. The most dangerous forms of corrosion are invisible.

MULTIPITCH BELAY ANCHORS

On multipitch sport routes you often see climbers with bizarre rigging at the belays. Using a simple pre-equalized setup minimizes the gear required, and increases the security of the rigging. If the positioning of the belay bolts is consistent from pitch to pitch, you can keep the sling tied and just clip it into each new set of anchors.

Pre-equalizing a double-length sling to build an anchor is simple, fast, secure, and uses little gear. Here the leader clipped one of the bolts as a first piece of protection.

Clipping to the bolts with the equalizer creates an anchor that splits the load equally between the bolts, even if the loading direction changes.

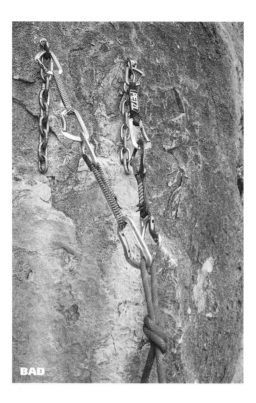

This setup wastes quickdraws, and it's actually a bit dangerous: the belayer needs to take care that the quickdraws do not unclip from each other every time he weights the anchors because of the carabiner-to-carabiner attachment.

SPORT ANCHORS EXERCISE

For New Sport Leaders:

Hang a quickdraw, get out your climbing rope, and practice clipping until you can do it smoothly and quickly every time. Practice with right and left hands, and with the gate opening right and left. Clipping well can save a few moments of fear for the leader and the belayer on those first leads.

For Intermediate Sport Leaders Aspiring to Multipitch Routes:

Find two bolts close together, or set two hangers into a piece of plywood. Clip both bolts with a double-length sling, pull two loops in the direction of loading, and tie the sling off to pre-equalize it. Now tie yourself in with a clove hitch or figure-eight-on-a-bight. Practice until you can rig the anchor in a few seconds.

CHAPTER 7

Traditional Belay Anchors

You awake to the familiar smell of pine, instantly aware that you're in Yosemite Valley. The route for today is the 15-pitch *Royal Arches*. Most of the climbing is easy, but to make good time you need to set belays fast and make quick transitions at those belays. You carry a good rack of wired nuts, hexes, and cams, along with webbing, cordelettes, quickdraws, and extra carabiners for rigging anchors.

The cracks are worn from thousands of passages, but the rock is solid and the anchors bomber. At each belay ledge you custom design the anchor, trying to be quick and keep the rigging clean. Trees make a quick anchor at some of the belays, while a combination of nuts, hexes, and cams—placed in old piton-scarred cracks—works at the other stations. When possible you save the cams for the next leader by using nuts, hexes, and natural anchors at the belay.

On the steeper pitches you always set at least three bomber pieces to hold a downward pull. In some situations you add an anchor to hold an upward pull, especially on pitches where the heavier climber is leading; or you might adjust the anchor for a sideways pull on the traversing pitches. When the three downward anchors aren't great, or if they're small pieces, you set more. But on the easy, low-angle pitches you sometimes cheat and only set two bomber anchors, or even use just one stout tree for the belay. Whether you're playing at your local crag or climbing the long, free classics of Yosemite, being able to quickly set a variety of simple, solid belay anchors is critically important.

This chapter covers:
- choosing where to belay
- rigging belays with a cordelette
- rigging with slings
- rigging with the climbing rope
- rigging with two ropes

- equalizing the load
- building upward-direction anchors
- creating multidirectional anchors
- rigging to a tree growing back from the cliff line
- extending from the anchor so you can see and communicate with your partner

Chapter 1 showed how to rig two- and three-point anchors with slings or a cordelette and discussed many important considerations of anchoring. Before you read on, it may be worthwhile to review chapter 1's discussion of pre-equalized and self-equalizing anchor rigging systems, as well as its coverage of equalization and V-angle.

A variety of methods for rigging three and four piece belay anchors are shown in chapter 1. It's almost silly how many different options you have for creating a belay anchor—there's no exclusive "best way" that fits all situations. What you want is a belay anchor that's strong, simple, and fast.

BELAY STATION

Usually the standard belay stances that most teams use are marked on the topo or described in the guidebook. You don't *have* to use the described belays; if you're climbing with a new climber it might be wise to shorten the pitches to facilitate communication and minimize rope stretch in a fall; if you're low on gear you also might stop short. If you're trying to climb fast you may blow past the standard belay to link up another pitch (or several pitches).

If the crack splits a large, clean wall (not cracked or detached on either side) and the rock is solid, you can set the anchors close together. If the rock is fractured or otherwise suspect, spread the anchors out to enlist multiple rock features. Never set all the anchors behind a single detached block or flake. Set the anchors high if possible so that the master point hangs at chest- to head-level.

CHOOSING YOUR BELAY STATION

A first-rate belay station has:

- fixed anchors or good cracks for building anchors
- safe positioning from rockfall
- a nice ledge for comfort and stacking the rope
- sight of the climber
- a position that minimizes rope drag for the last pitch and the next

You don't always get all of these qualities in a belay station. Foremost you want solid anchors and safe positioning. If you can't find good anchors or a good stance, maybe you can climb higher to find them. It's good for the belayer to sound the warning: "ten meters!" (or "thirty feet!") when that much rope remains, so the leader can start looking for a suitable belay. Once you find a good station, look around before setting the anchors. Avoid tunnel vision that focuses you on one solution only, unless that solution quickly meets all your needs.

BELAY RIGGING METHODS

As discussed in chapter 1, two good bolts or three bomber downward anchors make a good belay anchor. Having great individual pieces is the most critical aspect of building a belay anchor.

If the pieces aren't great and you can't find better ones, set more and equalize them—a four- or five-point anchor is not unreasonable if the pieces are small or mediocre. You can add an upward-pull piece to protect the an-

chors or belayer from getting pulled up if the leader takes a hard fall. Good lead protection just above the belay can almost be considered part of the belay anchors because it protects the anchors from a severe impact if the leader falls directly onto the belay.

Before building the anchors, analyze which direction the forces will come from, both while the second climber follows the pitch and when the leader climbs above. If the second's rope runs straight up to the belay, the anchors will get pulled down if he falls. If the leader is leading straight above the belay with no protection, the anchors will get pulled straight down with an extreme force if she falls. If she takes a hard fall after placing good protection, the belayer will get pulled toward the first protection, and the anchors might too. If the route traverses just before or just after the belay, the anchors can get loaded with a sideways pull. Build the anchor to be strong in any conceivable direction of pull.

Many options exist for rigging a belay anchor. The best method often depends on the team's climbing system and the number of climbers; sometimes it's dictated by what gear is left over at the end of the pitch; at other times it's a matter of personal preference.

If most of the rack is spent by the end of the pitch you may have to settle for a belay anchor that's less bomber than you want. You can add your body into the belay as shown in chapter 1, and once the second arrives with the cleaned gear you can bolster the anchors before anyone leads above.

A proliferation of bolted belays has

made anchoring easier, faster, and on some climbs, safer. Make sure the bolts are at least $\frac{3}{8}$-inch in diameter and tightly fixed. Back up the bolted belay with other pieces if you have any doubts about the bolts.

Climbers often take shortcuts—sometimes justifiable and sometimes stupid. With experience and education a climber develops good judgment, so any shortcuts are well thought-out. High-angle rock-climbing falls can create large impact forces, so you can't take too many shortcuts with the belay anchors without taking a huge risk.

Cordelette

A cordelette has multiple uses for anchoring and self-rescue. It's fast and simple for rigging three- and four-point belay anchors. A pre-equalized cordelette creates a convenient "work station" at the belay, with a top shelf and master point for clipping to the anchors. These clipping points are convenient if you have more than two climbers on the team. The cordelette works whether the pieces are close together or far apart, and it easily rigs multidirectional anchors. See chapter 1 for the steps to rig a cordelette.

The cordelette rigging method has come under some fire because it does not spread the load equally among the pieces, especially if the loading direction changes or if one leg is short. If you have bomber anchors equalization is not so important, because any of them can hold the maximum forces possible in a rock climbing fall. If the anchors aren't great (or you're not sure), or if the leader could take a high impact fall directly onto the belay anchors, a rigging method that equalizes the load better might be safer.

When used for rigging belays, the cordelette is first tied into a loop with a flat overhand, double fisherman's, or a triple fisherman's knot.

The belayer is tied into the master point while belaying a leader. The leader placed protection just above the belay to protect the anchors and the belayer from a high-force fall onto the belay. The belayer could be lifted several feet in a hard leader fall. Add an upward anchor closer to the belayer if you want to prevent this. Her belay gloves will make it easier to catch falls without burning her hands.

The guide's belay. The belayer is clipped into the top shelf of the cordelette and is belaying a second from the master point with an autolocking belay device so she'll never have to bear the weight of the climber on her harness. The master point is set high for convenient belaying. This system doesn't work well with a standard belay device.

Slings

Advancements in webbing material have created slings that are extremely light, compact, and strong. These new materials make it convenient to rig belay anchors with slings, allowing the climbing team to dump the heavier cordelettes. Rigging with slings also makes it easier to equalize the load among the pieces.

This clean arrangement uses only a double-length sling to equalize the load between the left cam and the two pieces on the right. The two extension-limiting knots make the clipping point of the sliding X redundant, and they allow for some directional shift while limiting extension if an anchor blows. An upward pull anchor is clipped with another sling to the master point.

To rig it, clove hitch a double-length sling to the lower right piece and clip the sling to the upper right piece. Pull the sling down, add the two limiting knots, and clip the left piece. Adjust the knots so they limit extension while allowing for some directional shift. Put a 180-degree twist in one of the webbing strands when you clip the anchor to make the sliding X. If the two right anchors aren't close together, use a sling to extend the higher piece.

Slings are frequently used to rig belay anchors, but often in a messy, gear-wasting fashion. A few nice solutions exist that are clean and efficient. The techniques shown in this chapter require only a sling or two and some carabiners for rigging three- or four-point belay anchors.

This is a reasonable anchor, but it's not as clean as the previous rigging. The upper two anchors are equalized with a sliding X, and an overhand knot minimizes extension if the highest piece fails. The upper two anchors are then equalized with the right anchor via a sliding X in a half-length sling (half the length of a shoulder sling to minimize extension if a piece fails). The lower clipping point is not redundant, so the rope was also clipped to the upper locking carabiner to back up the half-length sling. These placements in a horizontal crack will hold an upward pull, so no extra upward anchor is necessary.

A little slack between the clipping knots ensures that the lower carabiner gets loaded so it can equalize the force between all three pieces. As it's rigged, the two left pieces will hold 25 percent of the force, while the right piece holds 50 percent. If the load comes onto the upper tie-in, the left two pieces will hold the entire load and the right anchor will not contribute at all.

These four pieces are rigged with a four-loop sliding X using two double-length slings for redundancy. This rigging is fast, simple, and it equalizes the load among the four pieces, with each anchor holding around 25 percent of the load. If one piece fails, the slack disperses among the other three loops, so extension is minimal.

If the loading direction changes, the slings will shift in the clipping carabiner to maintain equalization. Using a large carabiner and thin Spectra (Dyneema) webbing makes it easy for the slings to shift. This setup doesn't work as well with fat webbing or tiny carabiners because friction prevents the slings from equalizing well. To rig it, clip both slings to all four pieces. Pull three loops down between the pieces (with both slings), put a 180-degree twist into each of them, and clip all four loops.

Rope

You can tie into all the anchors with the climbing rope for fast anchoring that requires minimal gear. Anchoring with the rope works well for a party of two who are swinging leads; with bigger teams, or if one person is leading all the pitches, it can be problematic getting climbers clipped in and out of the anchors because no master point exists. Tying the belayer's rope up in the rigging may also make it difficult to escape the belay in an emergency.

The old school method. One of the quickest and easiest ways to get into a series of anchors is to clip each one of them with a clove hitch. Cinch the clove hitches from bottom to top so all the anchors contribute, though it's impossible to distribute the load equally with clove hitches. This is fast when you're swinging leads, but it's hard to clip another climber into this anchor.

If you use the rope to rig anchors that are spaced horizontally, use the "triangle tie-in" to keep yourself tight to all of the anchors. The rope runs from the belayer up to the two left anchors, where it's tied into each with a clove hitch. Then it's tied to the right anchor with another clove hitch, and finally it runs back to the belayer's harness where it's tied with a fourth clove hitch. This rigging makes it easy to adjust the rope lengths so all of the anchors hold some of the load. The first protection was placed before the leader left the belay, so the belay essentially included four good anchors.

You could increase the strength of this belay anchor by equalizing the two left pieces. The lowest piece is a stopper which probably won't hold an upward pull. An upward pull anchor might be a good idea here, to protect the belayer and the lowest anchor from getting lifted in a leader fall.

CORDELETTE CRAFT

EQUALIZATION CONSIDERATIONS

You can rig the cordelette many different ways to bring the anchors together to a common master point. Several tricks exist for improving equalization, incorporating an upward anchor, or rigging anchors that are spread far apart.

Here the cordelette rigs four pieces set in a horizontal crack. This rigging should spread the load fairly evenly among the pieces because the leg lengths are all similar (unless the loading direction is different than anticipated). A clove hitch was tied into the rightmost piece, simply to keep the double fisherman's knot out of the way while the cordelette was rigged.

Three wired nuts and an Alien rigged with the cordelette. The Alien is set in a place where it can swivel to hold an upward or sideways load if needed, making the anchor multidirectional. The short leg going to the Alien may take most of the force, which may not be strong enough to hold a high-force leader fall onto the belay anchors. This anchor could be stronger if it was rigged to equalize the load among the pieces better.

The short leg here is clipped to two pieces equalized with a half-length sling. As long as all the pieces are good, this anchor will handle anything you can throw at it.

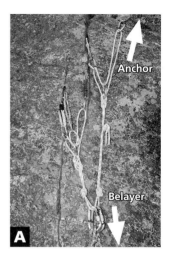

The equalizer rigging allows you to spread the load better among the pieces, but it's slow to rig. If any anchor fails, the other anchor on that side will prevent extension. This rigging puts 50 percent of the load on the right anchors, and 50 percent on the left anchors, but it's hard to spread the load evenly among the two right or two left pieces. Clipping into both strands of the master point with separate carabiners makes the rigging redundant. The carabiners can easily slide to adjust to the pulling direction to maintain equalization.

To rig this, clove hitch the two left pieces (the double fisher-man's knot was placed between these two pieces to keep it out of the way). Tie the two extension-limiting knots, clove hitch the two right anchors, and adjust the limiting knots and clove hitches so they sit where you want them.

A. This anchor looks like somebody's science project. It's slow to build, but it sure does equalize—this rigging will put roughly $\frac{1}{6}$ of the load on each of the three left pieces, and $\frac{1}{4}$ of the load on the two right pieces. If one piece blows the entire load will go onto the other side of the cordelette, though. Such complex systems don't have much place on long routes, though they can be fun for engineer-types who like to tinker (and maybe not-so-much-fun for their partners who have to wait around).

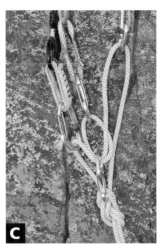

B. To rig this, tie a figure eight on a bight with a large loop in the cordelette. Clip a carabiner inside the top of the figure eight knot, and then wrap the loop twice through the carabiner to create three clipping loops.

C. Clip the loops into the three left anchors to equalize the load on them and tie the two extension-limiting knots.

D. Tie another figure eight on a bight with a large loop on the right side of the cordelette. Clip a carabiner inside the top of the figure eight. Clip the loop into both pieces, and then back down to the carabiner in the figure eight. This equalizes the load on these two pieces. Adjust the two extension-limiting knots, then clip into the two master point strands with separate carabiners, as shown in the first photo, to create a redundant, equalized anchor with minimal extension.

Sliding X

You can rig the previous anchor much more easily with one double and two shoulder-length slings. Triple equalize the three left pieces with a shoulder-length sling, and double equalize the right two pieces. Clip the double-length sling to one of the equalized slings, tie two extension-limiting knots, and then clip the double sling into the other equalized sling. Adjust the limiting knots, put a 180-degree twist into one of the clipping loops to make the sliding X, and clip in. The sliding X makes the master point redundant, so one clipping carabiner per climber works fine. Complex rigging like this is only necessary if you need to spread the load among a bunch of mediocre pieces like these microcams.

UPWARD-PULL ANCHOR BUILT INTO STATION

Upward anchors serve two purposes: to hold the belayer down, and to protect the other anchors from an upward pull. When it's important to hold the belayer down, an independent upward anchor, attached to the belayer as shown in chapter 1, usually works best.

You can incorporate an upward directional anchor into the rigging to create a multidirectional belay anchor that can withstand a pull in any direction. This can protect the anchors against an upward pull, and limit the distance the belayer can get lifted. The upward directional anchor should be the lowest piece.

Sometimes a cam set for a downward pull in a parallel crack is sufficient to counter the upward pull, because the cam will swivel and lock to hold an outward, sideways, or upward pull. However, in "wavy" rock the cam lobes might open up if the cam swivels; such a placement may not be reliable against an upward pull.

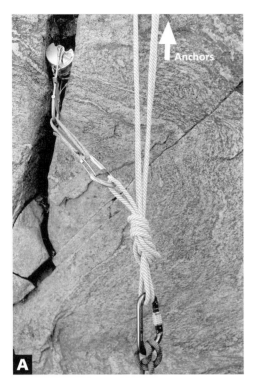

A. This anchor can handle an upward pull because the low cam will swivel to the new pulling direction. The leg going to the cam is short so this piece may feel most of the force if the leader falls directly onto the belay. This belay anchor is only good if the other two pieces are bomber, too.

B. When pulled upward the cam swiveled to confront the new pulling direction.

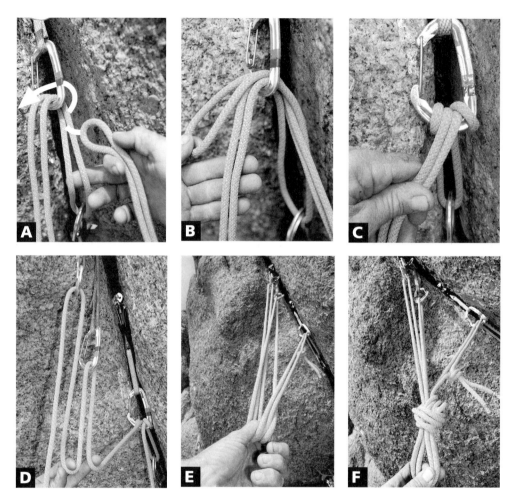

This rigging method cinches two opposing anchors tight against each other to actively hold the pieces in place and create a multidirectional anchor. You can also do this with a sling as shown in chapter 1.

A. Set four anchors in a crack. The lowest two should be opposing. Clip the cordelette loop into the upward-pull anchor, and clip both cordelette strands through the lowest downward-pull anchor.

B. Pass the opposite end of the cordelette between the two strands and through the upper carabiner again.

C. Pull the cord tight to cinch the pieces against each other.

D. Clip the cordelette loop to the remaining pieces and pull down a loop between each piece.

E. Pull all the loops in the expected direction of loading.

F. Tie the cordelette off with an overhand or figure eight to create the master point and top shelf.

A. You can also rig the same anchor by tying the opposing anchors together with clove hitches. You may as well set the knot that joins the cordelette between the two clove hitches to keep it out of the way while you rig.

B. This is a bomber, multidirectional belay anchor. The clove hitches work great for cams, but the cinching method shown above works better if you need active tension to hold nuts or hexes in place.

C. If the opposing anchors are close enough to each other, clip them together with a single clove hitch. This makes a convenient multidirectional setup, but it does not create active tension between the opposing pieces.

ANCHORS SET FAR APART

If one of the anchors is far above the others, you have a few options for extending it down. Following are three solutions for rigging the same set of anchors with a cordelette.

A. The cordelette can work for distant anchors if you untie the loop and tie a figure eight on a bight in each end. Clip one figure eight to the high anchor, the other to the low anchor, and clip the cord into the remaining anchors. In this case the lowest two pieces are wired nuts set in opposition to create a multidirectional placement. The nuts are clipped together with two carabiners (gates opposed) due to the three-way pull and possible cross-loading on the carabiner.

B. Pull the cord down in the direction of loading as normal and tie it off to create the master point. The extended cordelette works fine, but it does not provide a full-strength top shelf. With this rigging the highest piece probably won't share much of the load because the leg is so long and it's only a single strand which will stretch more easily than the two strand loops, but it's still there to serve as a backup.

A shoulder-length sling extends the high anchor, enabling the cordelette to connect all five anchors (including the two opposed nuts).

Here the lower anchors were rigged with a cordelette, and the climbing rope was extended to the backup anchor. The cordelette was shortened by tying a flat overhand knot to isolate some cord so the master point could be kept high.

If the backup anchor is really high, the climber might clip it directly with the rope and then downclimb back to the belay, top-roped by that piece. Then he would clip into the primary belay anchors and the rope coming down from the backup anchor to connect to all the anchors. Clipping with clove hitches allows you to adjust the rope to eliminate slack.

ADVANCED TIP—KEEPING THE MASTER POINT HIGH

Having the master point at chest- to head-level makes a convenient "work station." Here are three tricks for "shortening" the cordelette to keep your master point high if the anchors are close together.

This cordelette was used to clove hitch the lowest two pieces to oppose each other, which makes the anchor multidirectional. The third piece from the bottom is clipped twice, which uses more cord and keeps the master point higher. The double loops may give this piece more than its share of the load because that leg won't stretch as much as the others.

Tie another knot in the loop, farther from the ends of the cordelette, to shorten the loop and keep the master point high.

A. If you still have too much cord when it's time to tie off the cordelette, keep passing the cord around itself as you tie the figure eight.

B. The "figure nine" knot uses up much of the extra length of the cordelette.

TYING UP THE CORDELETTE

A. Spread your fingers to form a "spool." Grab to knotted side of the cordelette.

B. Wrap the cord repeatedly around your hand until you have a loop about 40- to 60-centimeters (16- to 24-inches) long remaining.

C. Wrap the loop that's left tightly around the coil. When there's only a small length of loop left, push it through the top of the coil.

D. Clip this loop to carry the cordelette.

MINIMALIST RIGGING WITH SLINGS

Many ways exist for rigging anchors with slings. These methods are great to know in case you drop your cordelette or use it for lead protection, or so you can leave the cordelette at home to save weight.

A shoulder sling and double-length sling combine to create three fixed legs, similar to a cordelette rigging. The shoulder sling was tied off with an overhand knot to shorten it. These anchors set in limestone are good but not bomber. They should be better equalized to get more strength from the anchor.

A double-length sling can rig a three-point anchor, if two of the anchors are in line with each other. The lower left nut clips just below a knot in the sling that eliminates the possibility of extension. The sling is pre-equalized, creating redundancy and a solid master point for the team to clip. While this method is fast and convenient for rigging bomber anchors, the first rigging with slings (shown at the beginning of the chapter) equalizes the load better.

If the belayer gets lifted she might pull out the low nut. An upward anchor could be clipped to the nut, the master point, or directly to the belayer to prevent this.

You can make minor adjustments in the length of a sling by wrapping it two, three, or more times through a carabiner. An overhand knot as shown above is better if you need to shorten the sling more than a little. Try to keep wraps closer to the carabiner spine than shown here.

A double sling with a sliding X and extension-limiting knot splits the load between the right anchor and the left two anchors. The higher left cam is clipped into the sling of the lower left cam to save gear, and the pieces are positioned to share the load. A lightweight locking carabiner on the lower left cam adds security, since it connects two of the anchors to the rigging sling.

The sling is not redundant in its master point. Tying another extension-limiting knot in the sling just below the left cams would make it redundant. You could also tie the rope into the second locking carabiner. An upward anchor can be clipped into the master point.

The equalized lower pieces comprise the primary anchor, with the highest piece serving as a backup. By tensioning the upper clove hitch more you can get all three anchors sharing the load. This isn't great but it's fast. It would be even faster if you eliminated the extension-limiting knots and used a half-length sling to equalize the left two pieces.

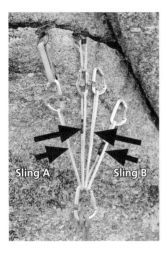  

Two shoulder-length slings each equalize two pieces—the slings were just the right length. If one of the slings needed shortening you could wrap it around a carabiner or tie a knot in the sling. If one anchor blows, or if the loading direction changes, the entire load will go onto just two of the anchors.

The top two cams are pre-equalized with a double-length sling. The knot creating the master point was adjusted so the hexagonal chock could clip into the master point and contribute to the anchor. Often you can slide the cam placements up or down to adjust the position of the sling. The hex looks like it might not handle an upward pull very well, though some crystals do hold it against an outward pull. You might add an upward anchor clipped to the master point or the belayer. This setup doesn't equalize great, but it's quick to rig and requires minimal gear.

The Darwin anchor. Climbers who set anchors like this will be removed from the gene pool. All of the pieces are set in a single detached flake, the hexes look like they could pull out easily, the rigging wastes quickdraws and carabiners, and it all relies on a single, non-redundant sling that doesn't even have a sliding X—if the left hex rips you get total failure. To top it off, the climber is clipped in using a clove hitch and a single non-locking carabiner. If the leader falls before setting good protection, this team is toast.

RIGGING WITH THE CLIMBING ROPE

It's fast to rig anchors with the rope, but it only works well for a team of two who are swinging leads.

ADVANCED TIP—MULTI-LOOP KNOTS

You can create multiple clipping loops in the rope by tying a dog-eared figure eight, a dog-eared bowline, or an equalizing figure eight. These methods use a fair amount of rope, so avoid them on rope-stretcher pitches.

The dog-eared bowline works well for clipping two anchors, such as this pair of bolts. Appendix 2 shows how to tie this knot, as well as the dog-eared figure eight, which also creates two clipping loops. This belayer is clipped into the bolts with two locking carabiners. The new lightweight locking carabiners don't add much weight to the rack, but they can add some extra security at the belay, though non-locking carabiners should be fine, too.

This bolted belay is nice because it has a third bolt for the leader to clip before setting off on the pitch. The bolt would be better if it was positioned a little higher. The belayer could also tie into this bolt if she was concerned about the quality of her two belay bolts.

The equalizing figure eight (see appendix 2) can adjust if the loading direction changes, though it may not give perfect equalization due to friction in the knot. As shown here, collapse one of the three loops to clip only two anchors.

You can clip three anchors with the equalizing figure eight. It's best if the anchors are good, and not too far apart, so the rope can't burn across itself if an anchor fails. You can tie an extension-limiting knot in the longest loops if you're concerned about that.

By making a bigger loop in the beginning and passing it through the figure eight one extra time, you can get four or five loops for clipping. Here four anchors are clipped and the fifth loop is collapsed.

To create a master point, tie a figure eight on a bight in the rope just below the multi-loop knot. You can belay the second directly from this master point if you have an autolocking belay device.

HALF ROPES

If you happen to be climbing with two twin, half, or single ropes, you can tie each rope to a different anchor cluster to make a quick belay anchor.

The lowest piece is a stopper which could get pulled out with an upward pull—an upward-pull anchor might be in order. This anchor could be strengthened by equalizing the two left anchors at the cost of a sling, carabiner, and a few seconds of time.

TREES

In some areas you can frequently tie off a tree to build an anchor.

Wrapping the rope around a stout tree and clipping it back to your belay loop makes an anchor with only one carabiner. Make sure the tree isn't covered in sap. You might want your belayer to be more than two years old.

Sometimes you want to anchor to a tree set back from the cliff's edge at the top of a route. One convenient method is to pre-equalize a cordelette around the tree and then clip your rope in with a locking carabiner and lock it. Now go back to the cliff edge and tie a clove hitch in the rope and attach it to a locking cara-biner on your belay loop. Lock the carabiner and cinch the rope up tight to fasten yourself to the tree. This rigging doesn't create a master point, so the climber is belaying directly off her harness belay loop.

You might want anchors at the cliff edge to back up the tree, prevent rope stretch, or give you directional stability (if the belay position is not in line between the tree and the climber). There are many ways that you could rig this. Here the belayer clipped the tree and went back to the cliff edge. Then she set the extra anchors, pre-equalized them, and clipped her rope into the pre-equalized sling. Finally she clipped the rope into her tie-in carabiner to connect the tree to the other anchors.

This climber was nearly out of rope but she wanted to belay close to the cliff edge to reduce rope drag and to communicate with her partner. The tree is set back from the lip, so she pulled up slack and clipped the rope into her harness belay loop with a clove hitch on a locking carabiner so she couldn't drop the rope. Then she rigged a sling around the tree, untied her original tie-in knot, and tied the rope's free end to the sling.

She belayed herself to the lip by feeding rope through the clove hitch. Then she set two pieces at the lip to backup the tree and to help keep her in position if her partner were to fall. She pre-equalized the two pieces and tied the rope into them. Finally she tied a figure eight on a bight to create a master point. She clipped her belay loop directly into the master point and rigged the belay device. After she was secure she untied the clove hitch that protected her while she rigged at the lip.

ADVANCED TIP—EXTENDING THE ANCHOR

Guides often extend themselves from their belay anchor so they can see and communicate with their clients. This is a great technique if your partner needs to be coached and the anchors are out of view of the climber.

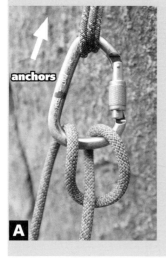

A. Set the anchors and clip the rope into the master point with a Munter hitch.

B. Move down to the belay spot, belaying/lowering yourself on the Munter hitch if necessary. Pull rope down to get some slack and tie an overhand in both rope strands. The overhand anchors you and creates a master point.

EXERCISE—BELAY ANCHORS

Find a safe, level place where you have access to some cracks. Set several belay anchors, and try rigging the same pieces with a cordelette, slings, and just the climbing rope. Use the minimal amount of gear to make a strong, redundant anchor. This doesn't mean taking short-cuts or setting sketchy anchors; it simply means rigging as cleanly and efficiently as possible. Try many of the different configurations shown in this chapter, to see what works well in different situations. Use a variety of cams, nuts, and other gear, and pay attention that the individual placements are solid. Have a guide or experienced climber evaluate your work.

C. You can do a direct belay with an autoblocking belay device off the master point.

D. If the terrain is tricky, you can belay the whole team back to the anchors by pulling the rope through the Munter hitch.

CHAPTER 8

Jeremy Medley on Trip Master Monkey *(5.12), Vedauwoo, Wyoming*

Trad Leading

Trad climbing can provide a lot of fun and adventure in wild, airy places. Whether you're monkeying out roofs in the Gunks, racing up Half Dome in-a-day, taking a voyage into the murky depths of the Black Canyon, climbing dreamy granite spires in the Bugaboos, or climbing at any of the other of hundreds of distinctive traditional climbing areas, one thing remains common: to lead trad routes safely you need good knowledge, judgment, and skills for protecting the climb. Every climb poses some risk to the leader; the goal is to manage that risk to an acceptable level, while enjoying the climbing.

This chapter discusses the rack you should carry on a traditional route and how to strategically protect a climb, balancing safety with efficiency. The chapter also covers:

■ setting the first piece in a pitch
■ protecting a pitch
■ using quickdraws and slings to minimize rope drag
■ using half ropes to reduce rope drag
■ the duties of a leader

Red River Gorge, Kentucky is famous for its relentlessly overhanging sandstone sport routes, but it also has some superb trad cragging. Say you're at "the Red," gearing up to climb the classic crack *B3* (5.11b). From the ground you can see that it's going to be mostly a finger and hand crack, but the crack appears to get smaller up high. Because it's only a one-pitch route, you cut the rack down to shave weight. A selection of wired nuts, micro nuts, a couple of hexes, some tiny cams, and a double set of finger- to hand-size cams will be more than sufficient.

The climbing goes smoothly, jamming the perfect crack in stellar rock. You set most of the pro from decent stances to save mental and physical energy for the crux. The climbing is pretty straight up, so you clip the cams and hexes directly, and you clip the nuts with a quickdraw. You set the nuts and hexes whenever the crack allows, keeping the precious cams in reserve.

The crack becomes less pro-friendly at the crux. You can guess that going into it, so you set two good pieces where the crack is still good, and you take a rest. Then you go for it—the pitch is sheer, with nothing to hit if you fall. You could try to wriggle in little nuts to reduce the runout, but that would take a lot of energy, and the pro wouldn't be good anyway. Better just to climb through. With the last cam well below your feet, you toss the rare trad dyno to slap the horizontal break. Once on this ledge, you get some reprieve before launching into the final, intricate moves. You set pro to keep yourself off the ledge in a fall, squeak through the awkward stemming moves, and clip the fixed tree anchor.

Using appropriate strategies is key for leading a trad route like *B3*. It's important to protect the route efficiently and safely, so you can manage the risk and conserve strength. It's also important to be able to set gear fast on steep trad routes.

Traditional racks. A big rack can be distributed between the gear sling and the harness, as with Charlie's rack (left). Lauri is the smart one. She's climbing a finger crack, so she has a petite rack that fits nicely on her harness loops. Kevin (right) has everything on gear slings—rack on the right, quickdraws on the left—so he can switch sides in the gnarly chimneys and off-widths that he loves.

On traditional climbs the leader needs quite a selection of gear for setting protection and building belay anchors. What you bring depends on the style and preferences of the climbing team and the requirements of the route. The rack described below is a good starting point for many multipitch traditional routes. It covers a range of crack sizes and provides plenty of slings, quickdraws, and carabiners for extending protection and setting belays.

- 1-2 sets of wired nuts
- 2-3 larger slung nuts
- 1-2 sets of cams ranging from $\frac{3}{8}$ to 3 inches
- 7-10 quickdraws
- 5-8 shoulder-length slings (those that easily fit over your shoulder)
- 1-2 double-length slings (twice the length of a shoulder-length sling)
- 6-8 extra carabiners
- 2-4 locking carabiners
- 2 cordelettes
- 1 gear sling (for carrying the rack, though some of it can go on your harness)
- 1 nut tool

This basic rack would get you up many routes. You might beef up the rack if the route has long pitches, and include some bigger gear if the climb has wide cracks. If you anticipate short pitches, or abundant fixed anchors, pare the rack down to save weight—it's much easier to climb with a light rack.

Seek information about recommended gear from a guidebook, other climbers, or by scoping the route from the ground. Bring a little extra gear if you have doubts about your information, and remember that cracks often look smaller than their true size when viewed from the ground.

PROTECTING THE CLIMB

Protecting a climb is part science, part art. You have a lot of creativity open to you, but you have to get a few basic things right. Having gear that's in good condition and well-organized by size on the rack will make the job easier.

The leader manages a fine line, using judgment to assess and mitigate risk, while climbing with confidence and efficiency. Some climbers overdo the analysis and protection, and it holds them back. Too many complicated systems or too much hesitation and doubt will climb a team right into the afternoon thunderstorm. To climb harder trad routes you need to be quick and confident with your protection.

FIRST PROTECTION

Once you get a few feet above the ground it's time to start setting protection. The first protection in a pitch can get a strong outward pull, depending on the position of the belayer. If this first piece pops out, the outward pull goes to the next piece higher—and it's possible to zipper out several pieces this way. To avoid this the first piece should be able to hold a downward pull to protect the climber, *and* an outward pull to protect the pieces above. A good cam, two pieces opposed, or another multidirectional anchor that can withstand an outward yank is a smart first piece.

On a multipitch route the leader should set good protection as soon as possible above the belay. This first piece of protection is one of the most crucial—it protects the belay anchors from a hard impact and it makes the catch easier for the belayer.

Depending on the arrangement of the anchor and your belayer, you can clip the top shelf for the first protection, or a higher anchor in the belay. Sometimes, especially when it's easy climbing above a good belay ledge, it's better to climb up a little ways to set the first protection.

If the first piece fails the outward pull, the other pieces may too, and they could "zipper" on up the rope.

While it's wise to clip protection early in the pitch to avoid a factor two fall onto the anchors, the jury is still out on whether it's smart to clip your belay anchors as the first piece of protection. While it should make the catch easier for the belayer, it also increases forces on the anchors by 60 to 70 percent because of the pulley effect. If the anchors aren't stellar you might not want to clip into them for lead protection.

You can clip the top piece in the belay. The individual anchors must be bomber for this to be safe.

Ahhh . . . that's better. Things get safer for the team once the leader sets solid protection above the belay. This reduces the fall factor, the impact force, and the pull on the belayer; and it protects the belay anchors from a high impact. The leader has to keep setting protection at reasonable intervals to continue reducing the fall factor and the potential force.

PROTECTING THE PITCH

The leader sets protection as the pitch unfolds. At the beginning of the pitch, set gear frequently to protect against a groundfall. As you get higher up the pitch, you can spread the protection out more, provided that there are no ledges to hit. Whenever you pass a ledge, protect closely again for a few pieces to keep you off the ledge if you fall.

When you get to a crux, set some good pro if possible. When the climbing is hard, more protection keeps you safer and keeps your head relaxed. It's smart to always have at least two bomber pieces between you and a bad fall, whenever a fall is possible. If the protection isn't great, place more.

If the rock is solid and the climbing is easy, you can get by with less protection, but you don't need to run it out too far. Making huge runouts is not heroic; it makes the entire team vulnerable to a broken hold or slip. Your partner counts on you to make good decisions and to get up the pitch, not get hasty, fall, and create an epic. Climbers who regularly push the limits of their ability and protection are rolling the dice. This may seem alarmist, but leader falls are the greatest cause of accidents in rock climbing according to *Accidents in North American Mountaineering 2004*, published by the American Alpine Club and the Alpine Club of Canada.

Set plenty of protection on traverses, especially before and after the cruxes—gear before the crux protects the leader, gear after the crux protects the second. If you've just climbed up a ways and are beginning a traverse, set a directional anchor to keep

Steph Davis cruising Quarter of a Man *(5.12), Indian Creek, Utah. Protecting the pitch involves using a good strategy for being both safe and efficient.*

the rope above the second climber through the vertical section. You can also set protection to show your partner where to go, or to keep the rope away from bad rock, sharp edges, or rope-eating cracks.

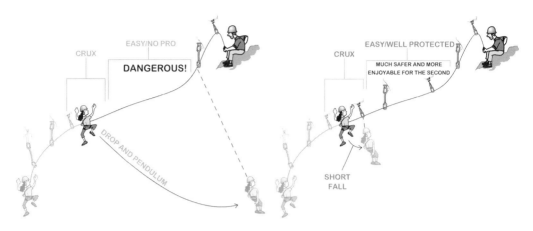

Set plenty of protection on traverses, especially after the cruxes, or else the second climber can take a big pendulum fall.

A clever leader will use protection to keep a rope from running into a tight crack, especially at the lip of a roof. Pro can be set to pull the rope away from the crack, as shown here, or it can be set inside the crack to keep the rope out. A nut, chock, or Big Bro—whichever fits the crack—works well for this.

DUTIES OF THE LEADER:

- Research the route's ascent and descent information, gear requirements, and current conditions
- Come prepared with the right gear and a good mental state
- Double-check knots, buckles, and belay setups before taking off on lead
- Set good protection right above the belay
- Climb efficiently and in control
- Set solid protection early and often in the pitch
- Stay aware of the ever-changing consequences of a fall, depending on ledges and the ground, and protect accordingly
- Exploit obvious protection opportunities, and ferret out obscure ones when necessary
- Stay on route
- Protect traverses for the second as well as the leader
- Use appropriate extension to keep the rope running straight, but don't over-extend the protection
- Avoid placing protection where it creates rope drag
- Try to keep the rope away from bad rock, sharp edges, and rope-eating cracks
- If the protection is sketchy or nonexistent, climb in absolute control or find a safe way to bail off the route
- Find a good belay station at the end of each pitch
- Watch the weather, and execute contingency plans if the weather goes sour or if the climbing is too hard or dangerous

EXTENSION

On a straight-up pitch it's usually okay to clip the rope directly into the slings of cams, or to clip wired nuts with a quickdraw. If the pitch traverses or climbs over a roof, however, it's good to extend the protection to keep the rope running straight. Try to get just the right length of extension—too much extension will increase the length of a fall more than necessary.

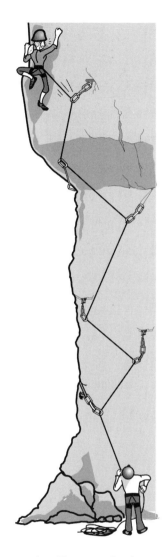 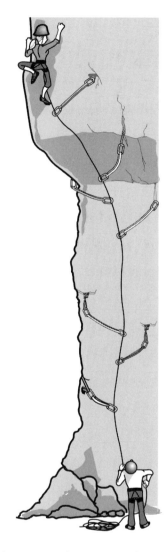

Poor extension. The protection is not extended enough, so the rope makes many bends back and forth. This creates huge rope drag and also puts a sideways pulling force on the pieces, which could pull them out in a fall.

Good extension. The rope runs clean by adding appropriate extension to the protection pieces.

On straight-up cracks it's quickest to clip a cam directly, if it's not buried deep in the crack. This also minimizes the length of a potential fall.

For just a little extension, to keep the rope running straight and decrease rope wriggle on the pieces, clip the protection with a quickdraw.

On this sharp turn right it's good to sling the protection extra long to prevent the rope from bending too sharply. A shoulder sling linked with a long quickdraw works here.

ADVANCED TIP—EXTENDABLE QUICKDRAWS

Extendable quickdraws are handy on alpine and traditional rock routes. When the route runs straight up you can leave the quickdraw shortened to minimize the length of a fall. When more extension is needed to keep the rope running clean, simply extend the sling.

B. Pass one of the carabiners through the interior of the other.

C. Clip the two loops of the sling.

A. Clip two carabiners into a shoulder-length sling and pull them apart onto opposite sides of the slings.

D. Now you have an extendable quickdraw.

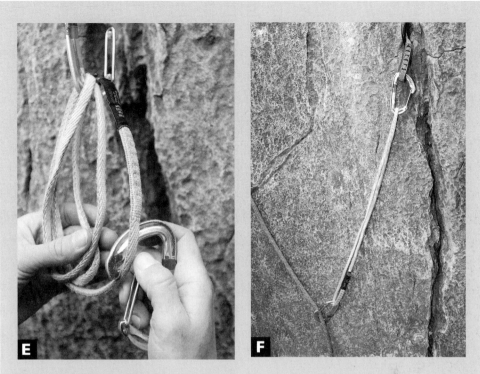

E. *You can quickly get full extension by unclipping any two strands . . .*

F. *. . . and pulling the sling apart.*

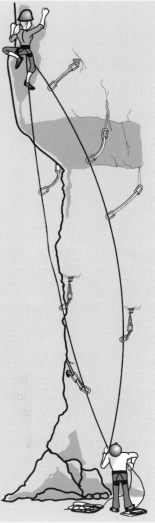

ADVANCED TIP—HALF ROPES

On wandering routes, half ropes work great for clipping selective pieces, one rope on the right and the other on the left, to keep the ropes running clean. If two ropes are needed to descend anyway, the half rope system can be the way to go. If the team must haul gear, though, a single rope and haul line works better.

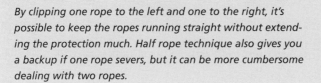

By clipping one rope to the left and one to the right, it's possible to keep the ropes running straight without extending the protection much. Half rope technique also gives you a backup if one rope severs, but it can be more cumbersome dealing with two ropes.

EXERCISE—TRAD PROTECTION

Beginning Trad Leader:

The safest way to start trad leading is to do a few mock leads, with a guide or *very* experienced trad climber cleaning and evaluating your protection. The assignment: perform four mock leads to see if you're ready to move on to the real deal. The first couple of leads should be easy, so you can relax while you set the gear. The next two leads should be progressively harder, to give you a feel of what it's like to place gear under pressure. If the climber or guide who evaluates your gear gives the green light, it's time to do some real leads. For your first climbs, choose routes with ample protection opportunities that are easy for you to climb, and slowly progress onto harder climbs.

Intermediate Trad Leader:

To choose the exercise, you should determine your climbing goals, along with your strengths and weaknesses. To improve your protection-setting skills:

Go to the base of an area that has plenty of cracks and set as much protection as you can in 10 or 15 minutes, and have your partner evaluate them. Set all the types of gear that you have on your rack; don't fall into the "cams only" mindset. Repeat the exercise in different spots until you can quickly set a variety of good protection.

If it's your climbing ability that you want to improve:

Top-rope and sport climb harder routes, boulder, and train in a climbing gym. Get a friend to drag you up some harder routes. Lay off on the ice cream and beer to get down to fighting weight, and try to climb at least three days a week (preferably outdoors, but indoors will help, too) to get fit and get your flow going. Work on climbing harder routes smoothly, and try to climb easier routes faster (on top rope). Watch good climbers to see how they move, and try to emulate their technique, confidence, and smoothness.

Experienced Trad Leader:

You get the most fun exercise, and it's one that you would do anyway. Get out and climb a bunch of routes, ideally including a diversity of rock types, short and long routes, and hard (but safe) routes that challenge your skill level. If anyone objects to all the time you're spending climbing, tell them it's an exercise from this book that will make you a safer, better climber. Most importantly, have fun!

CHAPTER 9

Tommy Caldwell going for a forty-footer on Broken Brain (5.12), Indian Creek, Utah

Climbing Forces

Climbing is bound by the laws of physics. Physics determines how a climbing move should be made, whether or not your foot will stick on a hold, and why a cam holds a fall. Physics also determines how much force is generated in a climbing fall.

This chapter discusses:

- Newton's Laws of Motion and how they relate to a falling climber
- how gravitational potential energy becomes kinetic energy, the energy of motion, in a fall
- how the belay method can drastically affect the impact forces in a lead fall
- what the fall factor is and how it influences impact force
- how the UIAA tests ropes to measure their impact force

For some climbers, enduring this chapter might be more painful than grinding up a feldspar-lined offwidth. If you find

---

THE RELEVANT LESSONS OF THIS CHAPTER

The highest impact forces on the protection, climber, and belayer occur if the leader falls close to the belay, with only a little rope out from the belayer to stretch and absorb energy.

Setting good protection early in the pitch, and regularly thereafter, significantly decreases the forces on the anchors, the climber, and the belayer in a fall. The early protection also backs up the belay anchors.

A "dynamic" belay, where some rope slips through the belay device when a fall is being stopped, can drastically reduce the force in a high-impact fall.

your eyes rolling up into your head, eyelids drooping, or your brain screaming for diversion, don't worry. Just read the sidebar on relevant lessons, drop the book, load your pack, and go climbing. If you're a true glutton, a student of physics, or just really bored, soldier on for a deeper understanding of climbing physics.

NEWTON'S LAWS OF MOTION

Newton pondered a falling apple. He may as well have considered a falling climber while devising his laws that define the motion of bodies:

The rate of acceleration of an object is proportional to the force applied to the object.

Gravity definitely seems to tug harder some days than others, but it actually pulls us toward earth's center with a constant force, equal to our body weight. In a free fall, gravity accelerates a falling climber's body at 9.8 meters per second^2 (32.2 ft/s^2): A body falls 4.9 meters the first second, three times further the next second, and five times further the third second. The body accelerates until it reaches terminal velocity—the speed where wind drag balances gravitational pull—after about five seconds.

A falling climber accelerates at 9.8 meters per second^2 until the rope arrests the fall. If the rope were a cable, the climber would halt almost instantly; the rapid deceleration would create a massive impact force on the climber and the protection, damaging the climber's internal organs and blowing out the climbing anchors. Dynamic climbing ropes stretch to control the climber's rate of deceleration, thereby limiting the impact force on the climber and the gear.

Every action has an equal and opposite reaction.

When we stand the ground pushes up with a force equal and opposite to our body weight. While climbing, the hand and footholds support a force equal to our weight (if we use the holds to oppose each other they support more than body weight). In a fall, the rope creates a force to catch us; this is called the impact force. The impact force on the rope pulls on the belayer, who must oppose the rope's pull. The top anchor holds a force equal to that on the climber and the belayer combined (if we ignore rope drag), and the rock surrounding the top anchor opposes the forces created by the anchor—hopefully—or else the anchor fails. The forces created in a lead fall begin with the falling climber, then transfer through the rope to the belayer, anchors, and ultimately the rock, to fulfill Newton's third law.

POTENTIAL AND KINETIC ENERGY

When climbing you perform work to move your body mass upward against gravity. Some of the energy used to climb becomes *gravitational potential energy*—energy stored due to the pull of gravity and your position above the earth. If you take a leader fall, potential energy quickly converts to *kinetic energy*—the energy of motion—as gravity accelerates your body downward. The farther you fall, the faster you go as your body's potential energy becomes kinetic energy.

Herein lies the double whammy of "running it out": a longer fall increases the chance of hitting something, and it increases the speed at which you hit it. The more speed you have, the more energy available to smash your bones if you hit a ledge.

Setting protection decreases the length and speed of a potential fall. The obvious conclusion: more protection means more safety . . . to a point. More protection also means more time spent fiddling with gear, more physical and mental energy devoured, and more gear carried. Every leader should seek a balance between safety and efficiency.

In a clean fall on a vertical or overhanging face with no ledges to hit, the rope absorbs most of the energy by stretching. Some energy also goes into overcoming rope friction from the carabiners and the rock, and perhaps lifting the belayer. If the impact force is high, some energy might go into forcing the rope to slip through the belay device and belayer's hand, provided that he's belaying with a device that does not lock the rope. If the fall isn't clean and the climber hits a ledge, much of the energy can go into breaking his bones.

When top-roping, a fall is halted almost immediately. A short fall creates less chance of hitting something, and it also transforms little potential energy into kinetic energy, so the speed of the fall is slow. This is what makes top-roping so safe.

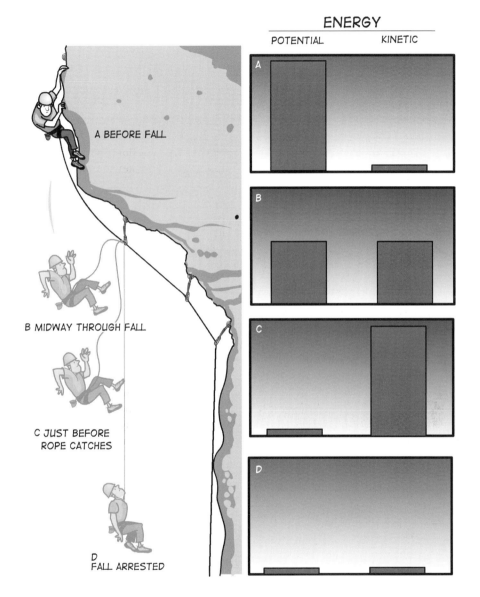

ENERGY

POTENTIAL   KINETIC

A BEFORE FALL

B MIDWAY THROUGH FALL

C JUST BEFORE
ROPE CATCHES

D
FALL ARRESTED

As you climb you store more potential energy. If you fall, the potential energy becomes kinetic energy, the energy of motion.

IMPACT FORCE

In a lead fall, the climber's body exerts an impact force on the rope that must be countered by the belayer. Friction at the high carabiner, and from the rope running over the rock and through other protection allows the belayer to feel less impact force than the leader. The force on the top protection equals the force on the climber and the belayer combined. The magnitude of the impact force created is largely determined by:

- belay method
- fall factor
- body weight
- rope elongation

BELAY METHOD

A *dynamic belay*, where some rope slips through the tube or plate belay device as the fall is stopped, arrests a fall more gradually. This can dramatically decrease the impact force in a fall with a high *fall factor*, which is explained next. The dynamic belay is usually unintentional—a belayer's hand can only hold so much force, so some rope automatically slips in a hard fall. A good belayer might also intentionally let some rope slip through the device if the climb is overhanging so the climber can not smack the wall.

If the belayer uses an autolocking device such as the Petzl GriGri or the Trango Cinch, the rope locks tight in a fall. If the belayer is also anchored tight, the belay will be almost totally static, and will create the highest impact force possible for that fall. Autolocking belay devices should only be used when the protection is bomber, such as on well-bolted sport climbs or trad routes

with perfect crack protection. Even on such routes, climbers should be aware that the impact force can be massive if the leader falls while close to the belay. On overhanging climbs a static belay can cause the leader to swing hard into the wall, a mistake that has caused numerous broken ankles.

If the belayer is on flat ground and using

The anchor and locking belay device creates a static belay, which can cause a high impact force on the anchors, climber, and belayer, especially if the fall factor is high. This could cause marginal pieces to pop, or the leader could swing hard into the wall if it's overhanging. In the worst case, a static belay could cause forces great enough to blow out a mediocre belay anchor.

an autolocking device, she can jump up as the force of the fall comes onto her. This is similar to having some rope slip through the belay device; it adds some dynamics to the belay, and decreases the impact force.

FALL FACTOR

$$\text{Fall Factor} = \frac{\text{vertical distance fallen}}{\text{length of rope out}}$$

The higher the fall factor, the greater the impact force in a fall. The important concept of the fall factor is that falls close to the belay create the highest forces because only a little rope exists between the belayer and the climber to absorb the energy of the fall. As the leader gets higher up the pitch, more rope comes into the system to stretch and absorb energy, so the force created in a fall decreases (provided that the leader has regularly placed protection).

The fall factor takes into account the amount of energy released in a fall and the length of rope available to absorb it. Two falls with equal fall factors theoretically create the same impact force, regardless of the distance fallen (if the rope, climber weight, and belay method remain the same). Obviously a longer fall might be more dangerous because of the increased chance of hitting something; but the forces generated are similar because the long fall has more rope available to absorb energy. The longer fall is also more severe because the force impacts the climber and anchors for a longer time.

A true factor 2 fall can only occur when the leader is directly above the belay on a vertical wall with no protection, so the fall is twice the length of the rope out. A factor 2 fall creates the greatest force possible on the climber and belayer if the belayer is using a device that allows minimal rope slippage, such as a Petzl Gri Gri or Trango Cinch. If the belayer is using a tube or plate device, rope will slip through the device, which in this case significantly decreases the forces, but could cause injury to the leader or burn the brake hand of the belayer. The force of such a fall comes directly onto the belayer and the belay anchors, making it a hard catch and creating an exceptionally high load on the belay anchors. Safe climbers avoid factor 2 falls by setting solid protection just above the belay. The first few pieces of protection in a pitch are critical because they decrease

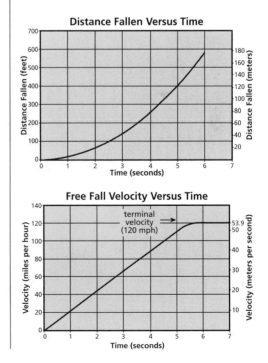

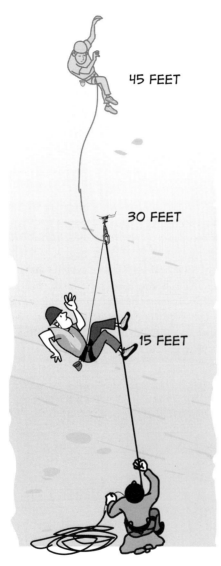

45 FEET

30 FEET

15 FEET

The fall factor is the distance that you fall divided by the amount of rope out. In this case a 30-foot fall on 45 feet of rope makes a fall factor of 0.67.

the fall factor and back up the belay anchors.

As you climb up a pitch more rope comes into the system. More rope means more capacity to absorb energy. A 10-foot fall 100 feet above the belay creates substantially less force than a 10-foot fall near the belay, because the rope stretches more.

BODY WEIGHT

On any given day your body weight is a fixed amount; gear and clothing add to your effective weight. Larger climbers create higher impact forces when they fall, so they might consider climbing on thicker ropes and placing extra protection or setting beefier belay anchors in some situations.

ROPE ELONGATION

A dynamic lead rope is really just a long spring. When a rope catches a fall, most of the kinetic energy goes into stretching the rope, and is ultimately dissipated as heat caused by friction between the rope fibers; some of the energy even transforms into molecular changes in the rope fibers.

As you climb higher up a pitch, the length of rope between the climber and the belayer increases. More rope out means more capacity for the rope to stretch and "absorb" energy, which results in a lower impact force, and a longer fall. Some ropes stretch more than others to give a "soft" catch; these low-impact-force ropes decrease the force on the protection, climber, and belayer, but the extra stretch might increase your chances of hitting a ledge.

As a dynamic climbing rope catches a fall the force on the climber, belayer, and anchors builds as the rope stretches. At the instant when the rope reaches its maximum stretch the load reaches its maximum impact force. Then the force diminishes until the top anchor holds only the climber's weight and some of the belayer's weight.

IMPULSE AND MOMENTUM

The *momentum* of an object equals its mass times its velocity. The faster an object is moving, or the heavier it is, the more momentum it has. If you graph the impact force as it grows and diminishes during the brief time that the rope arrests a climbing fall, the area under the curve equals the *impulse*, which is the change of a falling climber's momentum. You can calculate the impulse by multiplying the climber's mass by his *change* in velocity.

A falling climber slows from maximum velocity the instant the rope begins arresting the fall, to zero velocity once the fall stops. The *change* in velocity, therefore, equals the maximum velocity reached in the fall, because the final velocity is zero. In a clean fall, the length of the fall determines the maximum velocity.

Halting a fall creates a given impulse—equal to the climber's mass times the maximum falling velocity. As mentioned above, this equals the area under the force versus time curve. A static rope stretches little, so it stops a leader fall quickly. The rapid arrest drives the force to stratospheric levels, because less time slowing and stopping the fall means more force is required. In a fall onto a bungee cord, the huge elongation

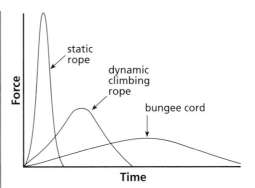

The static rope *doesn't stretch much in a leader fall, so the duration of the impulse is short, causing the impact force to spike. A* dynamic climbing rope *stretches enough to keep the forces reasonable, without dropping the climber too far. A* bungee cord *stretches so much that the time to arrest the fall is relatively long. This keeps the impact force low, but increases the length of the fall so much that the climber is likely to get battered on the way down.*

spreads the deceleration over a much longer time. The slow deceleration keeps the impact force low, but the impulse—the area under the force versus time curve—is the same as with the static rope. Bungee cords wouldn't work well for climbing, though, because falls would be too long.

A dynamic climbing rope is a compromise between the static cord and the bungee. It stretches just enough to keep impact forces in worst-case falls within a range that the human body can tolerate. A dynamic rope creates the same impulse to stop a falling climber as a static rope or a bungee, but creates much less force than a static rope, and stretches far less than a bungee.

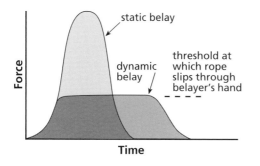

A dynamic belay increases the time to arrest the fall, thereby decreasing the impact force. A static belay halts the fall rapidly, creating a much higher peak force. The impulse is the same for either belay method, so the area under the force versus time curves is equal.

UIAA ROPE TESTS

The UIAA (Union of International Alpine Associations) conducts severe drop tests on ropes. These tests are much harsher than most real-life falls, so they provide a conservative measure of a rope's suitability for climbing. Before the impact test they condition each rope at a given temperature and humidity. During the test they drop an 80-kilogram mass 1.8 meters onto a 2.8-meter long piece of rope (the test mass starts above the anchor point). They drop the test mass repeatedly every five minutes until the rope breaks.

A single rope must hold at least five falls, and the first drop must not exceed 12 kN (2700 pounds) of impact force on the "climber." If the rope does not stretch enough, the impact force will be too high for the rope to pass the test. More importantly, if the rope doesn't stretch enough in a real fall, the impact force may damage the climber's internal organs and break the climbing protection. Each subsequent drop causes a higher impact force because the rope loses some of its elasticity. This is why it's smart to let your rope "rest" a few minutes after taking a high-impact fall.

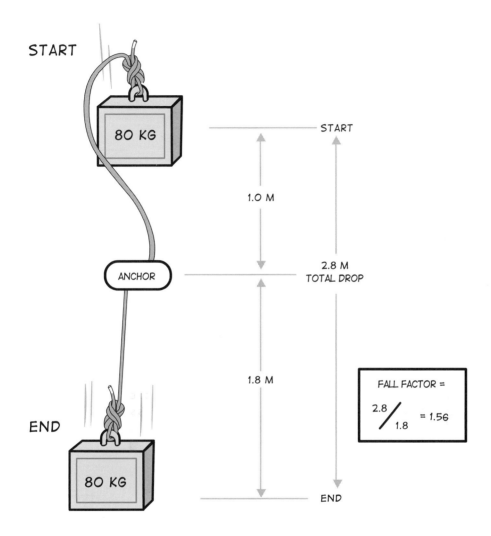

START

80 KG

START

1.0 M

ANCHOR

2.8 M
TOTAL DROP

1.8 M

END

80 KG

END

FALL FACTOR =

2.8 / 1.8 = 1.56

The UIAA drop test

STRENGTH OF CLIMBING GEAR

Climbing gear is designed to be functional, light, and to withstand climbing falls. The list below shows the range of strengths for various pieces of gear from different manufacturers.

CLIMBING GEAR STRENGTH RANGE	kiloNewtons	pounds
Nuts and Cams		
Micronuts	2-7	450-1575
Small wired nuts	4-7	900-1575
Medium wired nuts	6-12	1350-2700
Large wired nuts	10-12	2250-2700
Small cams	3-10	675-2250
Cams	12-14	2700-3150
Rope		4000-5000
Carabiners		
Full strength	23-25	5175-5625
Gate-open strength	7-10	1575-2250
Cross-loaded strength	7-10	1575-2250
Locking carabiners	23-30	5175-6750
High-strength Cord		
5.5 millimeter BlueWater Titan	14	3150
5.5 millimeter Beal Dyneema	17.7	3968
6 millimeter Sterling Powercord	21.3	4800
Nylon Cord		
5 millimeter Beal	5.7	1280
5 millimeter BlueWater	5.7	1283
5 millimeter Sterling	5.0	1134
6 millimeter Beal	7.4	1653
6 millimeter BlueWater	7.8	1755
6 millimeter Mammut	7.5	1688
6 millimeter Sterling	8.7	1955
7 millimeter Beal	10.3	2315
7 millimeter BlueWater	11	2475
7 millimeter Mammut	10	2250
7 millimeter Sterling	14.3	3210
Webbing Slings		
8 mm Mammut Dyneema	22	4950
12 mm Mammut Dyneema	22	4950
12.7 mm (½") Sterling Spectra	16.4	3690
17.4 mm (¹¹⁄₁₆") Sterling nylon	22.6	5100
12 mm Black Diamond Spectra	22	4950
18 mm Black Diamond nylon	22	4950
Daisy chain		
18 mm Black Diamond nylon	16	3600
12 mm Black Diamond Spectra	19	4275

EXERCISE—PETZL FALL SIMULATOR

The French climbing company Petzl has designed a "fall simulator" that is accessible on their website (*www.petzl.com*). With the fall simulator you can plug in certain variables, such as the belay technique, the type of protection, the weight of the leader, the diameter of the rope, and the distance the leader is above the protection and the belay, and you'll get back theoretical impact forces on the climber, belayer, and top anchor.

Although the fall simulator's calculations for impact force are extremely simplified compared to reality (and in some cases you may get significant errors), it's still enlightening to change the variables around and see how this affects the impact force. That's the exercise. Plug in your body weight and the size of rope that you use, and then change the belay method, length of fall, distance above the belay, and type of protection to see how the impact force changes.

Appendix 1: Webbing, Cord, and Carabiners

Webbing, cord, and carabiners are used for rigging climbing anchors. It's important to have the right material for the job.

CORD AND WEBBING

Cord is available in nylon and high-strength materials. With nylon, use at least 7-millimeter diameter cord for anchoring. This is probably the best material for anchor cordelettes, except that it's a little heavy and bulky. The ultra-high strength cords are suitable in diameters of 5.5 millimeters. When buying a cordelette, about 4 meters (13 feet) of cord makes a good rescue cord. 5 to 6 meters (16 to 20 feet) is a good length for building anchors.

Webbing comes in nylon and varying thicknesses of Spectra (know as Dyneema in the European products). Nylon grips better for making friction hitches in emergency situations, but the thin Spectra slings are compact and light. Full-size knotted webbing slings are fading in popularity—sewn slings are stronger, less bulky, and cannot accidentally untie.

Soft goods such as the nylon or Spectra in cords, slings, harnesses, and ropes are susceptible to gradual weakening from ultraviolet exposure, and even rapid weakening from chemical contamination, especially battery acids. For that reason you want to take good care of your climbing gear. Don't toss it in a messy car trunk; rather, store it in a dry, dark, clean place.

CARABINERS

Climbers use carabiners for multiple purposes, including:
- clipping into belay and rappel anchors
- clipping the climbing rope into lead protection

- rigging a belay/rappel device
- carrying equipment on the harness or gear sling
- connecting gear to the rope for hauling

SHAPE

Carabiners come in many shapes and sizes.

Oval carabiners work great for racking wired nuts. They put equal loads on the spine and gate so they are weaker than D-shaped or asymetrical carabiners (because the spine is stronger than the gate).They are also larger and heavier than more modern designs.

D-shaped carabiners concentrate the force on the carabiner's spine for increased strength.

Asymmetrical carabiners put the load on the spine and have a large gate opening for easy clipping.

The shape of a carabiner's cross-section helps determine its strength, weight, and the radius of its rope-bearing surface. A smaller radius carabiner can severely stress the climbing rope by bending it too sharply under load. Carabiners with a round cross-section require more mass of aluminum than other carabiner shapes to provide a given strength. An oval cross-section allows a slightly lighter mass to provide the same pulling strength, though you lose some strength if the carabiner is loaded sideways. Modern carabiners with I-shaped, T-shaped, and hourglass cross-sections place the aluminum mass where it provides great strength and an ample rope-bearing surface.

STRENGTH

Carabiner spines are stamped with three strength ratings. (If your carabiners are not stamped, retire them and buy new ones.) The strength is labeled with the following symbols:

- ↔ **Closed-gate strength:** A carabiner is by far strongest when loaded along its spine with the gate closed.
- ◡ **Gate-open strength:** A carabiner with its gate open can lose two-thirds or more of its strength.
- ↕ **Cross-loaded strength:** A cross-loaded carabiner, with the weight pulling outward on the gate also loses two-thirds or more of its strength.

A rack of super-light carabiners can save a lot of weight, but be careful: Some light carabiners post high strength ratings in the lab tests, but tweak them sideways and they are not very strong. Other light carabiners are so small that they're hard to clip. The best ones work great, and they can slice a good deal of weight from the rack.

GATE

Carabiners come with several types of gates. A carabiner gate should be easy to clip, and it must provide strength when the carabiner is closed. One end of the carabiner gate has a hinge upon which the gate rotates, and the other end has some sort of closure for connecting the gate to the carabiner when it's closed. This connection is a crucial component of the carabiner's strength—without it, a closed carabiner will be no stronger than a carabiner with its gate open.

Solid gate. For many years all carabiners came with a straight solid gate, and many excellent modern carabiners still have solid gates. One possible disadvantage of the solid gate is that in a fall the mass of the gate can cause it to vibrate open and closed. If the load comes onto the carabiner with the gate open it can break. This is rare, but it occasionally happens.

Bent gate. Bent gate carabiners make it easier to clip the rope in. These carabiners should be used only on the rope-end of quickdraws.

Wire gate. Wire gates are strong, light, easy to clip, and less prone to vibrate in a leader fall, which decreases the chance of breaking a carabiner.

Pin-and-notch. Traditionally, the carabiner gate has a pin that closes into a notch in the carabiner. If the carabiner is severely loaded, the pin locks into the notch to provide strength at the gate. The notch sometimes snags on the wire cable of nuts, which can be inconvenient.

Keylock. The keylock gate closure provides a strong, clean closure with no notch to snag on gear.

LOCKING CARABINERS

Locking the gate on a carabiner prevents the gate from accidentally opening and unclipping. Locking carabiners are used for many crucial clipping points, including:

- clipping into anchors
- rigging belay or rappel devices
- clipping a haul rope to the harness
- attaching a pack to a haul rope
- clipping crucial lead protection

Locking carabiners are available in three different gate designs. Which to use depends on your personal preference.

Screw gate. You spin the locking collar to lock a standard screw-gate carabiner, and spin it the opposite way to unlock it. For a secure lock spin the collar until it cannot spin any farther (not just part way down). Screw-gate carabiners are convenient because you can easily clip them when they're unlocked, but you have to remember to lock them when you need security. Make a habit of locking the gate immediately after clipping it.

Autolocking. Autolocking carabiners have spring-loaded gates that lock automatically whenever the gate closes. They are great for new climbers and those who often forget to lock their carabiners. Some climbers prefer the autolocking feature, while others find it a nuisance when trying to clip the carabiner. It is possible for the autolock gates to open if a loaded rope runs across them.

Button-lock. Button-locking carabiners lock automatically when you twist the gate. To unlock them, push the button and spin the gate. This design makes it difficult for the carabiner to accidentally unlock, but most climbers don't find it as convenient as a standard screw gate.

SHAPE

Locking carabiners come in a few shapes. The original "lockers" were D-shaped and oval, though now the asymmetrical and pear shapes are more popular. It's nice to carry some small, lightweight locking carabiners for applications that do not require a big gate opening or large interior space. The large pear-shaped HMS locking carabiners work well with a Munter hitch for belaying or rappelling without a device, and their larger size makes them easy to handle. (HMS come from German *halbmastwurf sicherung,* which means "half Munter hitch.")

CARE

Inspect your carabiners periodically. If you find notches or grooves in them (which can result from contact with sharp bolt hangers or erosion from rappelling or repeated lowering) retire them. If a carabiner gets dropped a long way, toss it out (chances are it's still fine, but you don't want to learn otherwise by taking a huge fall when your carabiner breaks!).

Many bolt hangers have sharp edges, which can be hard on carabiners, especially when you are working sport routes. If a carabiner becomes gouged, retire it.

If the gate on a carabiner gate becomes sticky, lubricate it. Use a Teflon spray lubricant, or the lubricants sold for camming devices, because they attract less dirt. If it's still sticky, discard the carabiner—it's dangerous if the gate does not close every time you clip the carabiner.

QUICKDRAWS

Quickdraws are the workhorse of sport climbers. Sport draws ideally have a bent gate carabiner on the bottom that is fixed from rotating, and a standard gate carabiner on the top. Good sport draws are somewhat stiff for easy clipping. Quickdraws for traditional climbing can be the same sport draws with a few extendable quickdraws tossed in, or another set of lighter, more pliable draws. Inspect the webbing for wear and the carabiner for notching (especially the top one that gets gouged by bolt hangers).

Appendix 2: Knots

Climbers use knots for many purposes. This section focuses on knots used by climbers to construct anchor systems and attach themselves to the anchors. Other climbing knots are not included—see *Rock Climbing: Mastering Basic Skills* and *Knots for Climbers*, both by Craig Luebben, or Clyde Sole's *The Outdoor Knots Book* for more climbing knots.

When reading the knot descriptions, the free end is the end of the rope, while the standing end refers to the side with most of the length of the rope. A bight is a loop of rope that does not cross itself, while a coil is a loop that does cross itself. When tying knots, keep them tidy and free of extra twists so they maintain full strength and they're easy to visually check.

Some knots weaken the rope more than others because they bend the rope in a tighter radius. This creates shear stress in the rope (loading across the rope fibers rather than along their length), and can severely stress the rope on the outside edge of the bend. The figure eight is a strong knot for tying into the rope because it does not bend the rope sharply. Many climbing books include a chart to show the relative strength of various climbing knots. These numbers are only roughly accurate, and they change with the material and diameter of the cord.

KNOTS FOR TYING INTO THE HARNESS

FIGURE EIGHT TIE-IN

This is the standard knot for tying the rope to your harness because it's strong, secure, and easy to visually check.

A. Make an "eight" in the rope 2 or 3 feet from the end.

B. Pass the end of the rope through the tie-in points on your harness, which usually include the leg loops and the waist belt.

C. Retrace the eight with the end of the rope.

D. Continue retracing the eight.

E. Keep the knot "well-dressed." Avoid extra twists, and make the tie-in loop small so the knot sits close to your harness. Cinch all four rope strands tight to secure the knot.

A properly tied, well dressed, and tightly cinched figure eight knot does not require a backup knot unless the rope is especially stiff. Nonetheless, it's not a bad idea to add a backup to your tie-in knot.

GRAPEVINE BACKUP

Many climbers tie a backup knot that protects the primary knot from untying. Some use a simple overhand, but the overhand often unties itself within a single pitch of climbing. Use a grapevine or extra pass to back up your figure eight knot.

A. Tie a grapevine knot to back up the figure eight. Coil the rope once around its standing end, then cross over the first coil and make a second coil.

B. Pass the rope end through the inside of these coils and cinch the grapevine tight. Leave a 2- or 3-inch tail in the end of the rope.

EXTRA PASS BACKUP

The extra pass is simple: pass the rope end one more time through the figure eight knot to secure it.

C. Tie a figure eight knot, then pass the rope end one more time through the figure eight.

D. This secures the figure eight.

KNOTS FOR TYING INTO ANCHORS

Always use a locking carabiner for tying into anchors. Lacking a locking carabiner, you can substitute two carabiners with gates opposed (facing opposite directions).

CLOVE HITCH

The clove hitch allows you to adjust the length of your tie-in to the anchors without untying or unclipping the knot. To extend or shorten your tie-in simply feed rope through the clove hitch. Once you unclip the clove hitch, it's gone—no knot to untie. Always cinch the clove hitch tight by pulling on both rope strands or it can loosen and possibly unclip itself from the carabiner.

Forming the two loops and clipping them into the carabiner is the fastest way to tie the clove hitch. You can also tie the clove hitch one-handed. Both methods are shown.

When belaying a lead climber tie the clove hitch with the load strand next to the spine of the carabiner for maximum strength. The carabiner can lose up to 30 percent of its strength (depending on the carabiner shape and rope diameter) if the load strand sits near the carabiner gate. This is not a problem if the carabiner only holds body weight, but it could be dangerous if the attached belayer catches a leader fall.

A. Twist two coils into the rope so it looks like a two-coil spring.

B. Slide the top coil below the bottom coil. Do not twist or rotate the coils.

Load strand

C. Clip both coils into a locking carabiner and lock the gate. If you'll be belaying a lead climber, be sure that the load strand of your rope sits next to the spine of the carabiner.

To Tie a Clove Hitch One-handed:
Sometimes you need to hold onto the rock with one hand while you tie the clove hitch with the other.

A. Clip the rope into the carabiner. With the carabiner gate facing you, pull one strand of rope behind the other.

B. Twist a coil into the rope (twisting toward the carabiner gate rather than away from it).

C. Clip the coil into the carabiner. If you twisted the rope correctly you get a clove hitch; if not, you get a girth hitch. Try again.

D. Lock the carabiner.

OVERHAND

The overhand knot is useful for creating a loop. Because it puts a sharper bend in the rope, it's not quite as strong as a figure eight knot, and it's harder to untie after being heavily loaded.

A. Take a bight of rope and make a coil in both strands of the bight.

B. Pass the bight through the coil.

C. Cinch the overhand tight.

FIGURE EIGHT ON A BIGHT

Tie a figure eight in the middle of the rope to make a strong loop for clipping yourself into anchors. The figure eight on a bight works in many situations where you need a secure loop to clip. It is easy to untie even after loading.

A. Take a bight of rope and form an "eight" with the two strands of the bight.

B. Pull the bight through itself, cinch the figure eight tight, and clip it.

DOUBLE LOOP FIGURE EIGHT

The double loop figure eight creates two secure loops that can be clipped to two different anchors. It is not truly redundant, because if one loop severs, the other loop may slip through the knot, causing anchor failure. However, the rope is rarely redundant anyway. Make sure the rope does not contact any sharp edges.

A. Begin tying a figure eight on a bight, with a longer than normal loop.

B. Rather than passing the initial bight through the eight to finish the knot, pass a bight from each strand through the figure eight.

D. Pull the resulting bights through the figure eight to cinch the knot tight.

C. Take the initial bight and flop it over the entire knot.

E. Adjust the loop lengths by pulling the rope through the figure eight. This lengthens one loop and shortens the other.

DOUBLE LOOP BOWLINE (ALSO CALLED BOWLINE ON A BIGHT)

This knot also creates two loops for clipping into a pair of anchors. It's a bit quicker to tie than the double loop figure eight, and uses a little less rope. It is more redundant than the double loop figure eight when tied correctly and cinched tight.

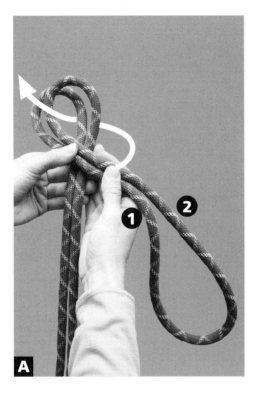

A. Take a bight of rope and make a coil with both rope strands.

B. Reach through the coil and grab rope strands 1 and 2. Pull strands 1 and 2 through the coil as shown.

C. Flop the overhand loop over the rest of the knot.

D. Pull rope into strands 1 and 2 to create two loops, while collapsing the original overhand loop. Adjust the lengths of the two loops by pulling rope through strand 3. This lengthens one loop and shortens the other.

EQUALIZING FIGURE EIGHT

The equalizing figure eight knot can equalize the load on two or three anchors, but it uses a lot of rope. Don't use this knot if the next pitch is a rope stretcher. The equalizing figure eight is not redundant; keep the loops away from sharp rock.

A. Tie a figure eight on a bight with a large loop.

B. Pass the loop back through the figure eight.

C. This creates three loops for clipping into three anchors.

D. Collapse one loop for clipping into two anchors.

KNOT FOR TYING A ROPE AROUND A TREE OR BOULDER

DOUBLE BOWLINE

The double bowline is great for tying a rope around a tree, boulder, or other natural an-chor. Many sport climbers also use a double bowline for tying in because it's a snap to untie, even after multiple falls. The double bowline sometimes unties itself, especially if the rope is stiff—always back up the double bowline with a grapevine or other secure backup knot and cinch both knots tight.

A. Pass the rope around a tree or other anchor, then twist two coils in the standing end of the rope.

B. Bring the free end of the rope up through the coils, down around the standing end of the rope, and back down through the coils. The rope's free end should come into the middle of the double bowline.

C. Cinch the double bowline tight.

D. Finish the bowline with a grapevine backup.

KNOTS FOR JOINING WEBBING OR CORD

WATER KNOT

Water knots tie pieces of webbing into loops. The water knot unties over time as it gets loaded and unloaded—check that the tails are at least 7 or 8 centimeters (3 inches) long every time you climb. Some climbers tape the tails to prevent them from creeping. If you do this, leave the ends of the webbing in view so you can see them.

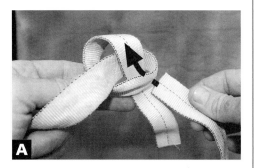

A. Tie an overhand knot in one end of a sling and match the other end of the webbing to the first end.

B. Retrace the original overhand knot.

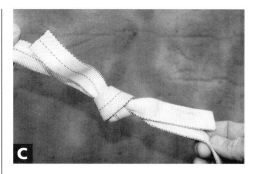

C. Cinch the knot tight. The tails should be at least 3 inches long.

FLAT OVERHAND

Many guides use the flat overhand for tying a cordelette into a loop because it's quick to tie and untie. The flat overhand is more secure than it appears, provided that you cinch it super tight and leave the tails at least 10 centimeters (4 inches) long. When using the flat overhand to join rappel ropes, leave the tails 30 centimeters (12 inches) long. A double fisherman's knot is stronger than the flat overhand, making it a better choice when the cordelette is used in a single loop, for example to tie off a tree or boulder. If the cordelette is used to rig a three-point (or more) anchor, then the flat overhand only supports one leg of the cordelette, so it's sufficient. If one of the anchors isn't bomber, put the knot in that leg to keep the weaker links together.

A. Take both free ends of the cordelette and tie an overhand knot.

B. Cinch the knot tight, leaving the tails at least 10 centimeters (4 inches) long for cord and 30 centimeters (12 inches) long for rope.

C. Tie a second overhand in one or both of the tails to increase the knot's strength and security.

D. This rope is now rigged for rappelling.

DOUBLE FISHERMAN'S

The double fisherman's knot joins cord into a loop, for example to close a cordelette or sling a chock.

A. Coil one free end of the cord around the other.

B. Cross the cord over itself and make a second coil.

C. Pass the end through the inside of the coils.

D. Repeat the first step, this time coiling the second rope around the first, but in the opposite direction so the finished knots are parallel to each other.

E. Cinch the knots tight. When the knot is finished the coils should be clean and parallel as shown.

TRIPLE FISHERMAN'S

Add one more coil to the double fisherman's and you get a triple. Some high-strength cords require a triple grapevine because they are slippery. Check the manufacturer's recommendations.

A. Coil the free end of one rope three times around the second rope, crossing over the first coil to make the second and third coils. Pass the end through the coils.

B. Repeat the first step, this time coiling the second rope around the first, but in the opposite direction so the finished knots are parallel to each other.

KNOTS FOR ATTACHING SLINGS

GIRTH HITCH

The girth hitch has many uses. With a girth hitch you can:

- fasten a sling or daisy chain to your harness for clipping into anchors (always tie into the anchors with the climbing rope if you will be belaying)
- fasten a sling around a tree to make an anchor
- attach two slings together to make them longer
- connect a sling to a carabiner without opening the carabiner's gate (perhaps because it's your only attachment to the anchor)

Don't girth-hitch the cable on a nut or chock, or any other small diameter object, because the sling may be cut by it under load.

In a recent incident, a thin dyneema sling that was girth-hitched to another sling broke under body weight. The sling may have been compromised, but climbers may wish to avoid girth-hitching thin slings together.

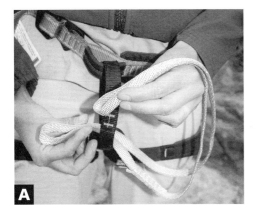

A. Pass the webbing sling through your belay loop, or around any object you want to fasten it to, and pull one end of the webbing through itself to create the hitch.

C. You might girth-hitch two slings to your harness so you can clip them into separate anchors, or clip both into the anchor master point for redundancy.

B. This fastens the webbing to the belay loop.

FRICTION HITCH

PRUSIK

If you're only going to know one friction hitch, the Prusik is it. It's easy to remember and it grips well.

A. Take a thin-diameter cord (5 to 7 millimeters in diameter) tied into a loop, wrap it once around both strands of the rappel rope and pass it through itself as if you're making a girth hitch.

B. Wrap the cord once again around the rope and through itself.

C. A 2-wrap Prusik.

D. Repeat the above procedure to create a 3-wrap Prusik for more friction. Keep the wraps neat and parallel.

AUTOBLOCK

The autoblock adds convenience and safety by backing up your brake hand when rappelling. If you accidentally let go of the rope the autoblock "grabs" the rope and halts your descent. The autoblock prevents overheating your brake hand on a long steep rappel because your hand rests on the autoblock, not the sliding ropes.

The autoblock is usually set on the harness leg loop so it cannot touch the belay/ rappel device. If the autoblock tails are too long, or if the rappel device sits too low, the cord can touch the device. In this case it may not lock, or worse, it could jam in your rappel device, stranding you until you unweight it. If you can't get the required separation between your autoblock and rappel device, extend the rappel device farther from your harness by girth-hitching two short slings into your belay loop and attaching the rappel device to them.

Clip a nylon sling (⁹/₁₆″ wide or less) or a loop of cord (5 to 7 millimeters long) to your leg loop with a locking carabiner. Wrap the sling or cord around the rope.

Far left: Wrap it four times until you have a 5- to 7.5-cm (2- to 3-inch) tail on each end.

Left: Wrap the cord too tight and you'll have a slow, jerky rappel; not tight enough and the autoblock won't grab when you need it. Practice with the autoblock to get the length right. The rappel device goes on the rope above the autoblock.

Appendix 3. Equations

We omitted scientific equations in the text to make the discussion of climbing physics less confusing. For those who care, the following equations relate to material in chapter 9, Climbing Forces.

$F = ma$ F = force, m = mass, a = acceleration

$W = mg$ W = weight, g = acceleration due to gravity (which is constant at the earth's surface)

$E_p = mgh$ E_p = potential energy, h = height (length of a potential fall)

$E_K = \frac{1}{2}mv^2$ E_K = kinetic energy, v = velocity

$P = mv$ P = momentum

$I = P_{initial} - P_{final}$ I = impulse, $P_{initial}$ = momentum before the rope begins to arrest the fall, $P_{final} = 0$ (momentum after the fall has been arrested)

$I = m(v_{max} - v_{final})$, v_{max} = maximum falling velocity, $v_{final} = 0$ (velocity after fall has been stopped)

$v_{max} = (2gh)^{1/2}$ the potential energy at the beginning of a free fall equals the kinetic energy as the rope begins to arrest the fall, which allows us to calculate the maximum velocity of the falling climber

$I = m(2gh)^{1/2}$ the impulse required to arrest a fall is determined by the falling climber's mass and the length of the fall

Glossary

aid climbing Pulling on protection or climbing upward while standing in slings attached to anchors. Used to bypass sections that the team cannot free climb

American Triangle An anchor rigging that increases the force on the individual anchors. It is created by threading the webbing or cord through two anchors and tying the ends together, forming a triangle that causes the anchors to pull against each other; the larger the angle in the triangle's bottom corner, the greater the forces. Dangerous if the anchors are not bomber; it is commonly found on fixed rappel anchors

AMGA American Mountain Guides Association, a national nonprofit organization that promotes high standards for guides. AMGA trains and certifies guides in rock guiding, alpine guiding, and ski mountaineering guiding, and accredits guiding companies.

anchor Any temporary or permanent attachment to the rock used to protect a climber against a fall, fix a team to a belay, or fix a rappel rope. A good anchor can hold several thousand pounds, a bad anchor may crumble under body weight. Anchors come in many forms, including trees, boulders, chockstones, pitons, bolts, nuts, hexagonal chocks, camming devices, expandable tubes, and more.

autoblocking belay device A belay device for belaying a second climber that locks the rope automatically in a fall; i.e., the Kong GiGi, Petzl Reverso, and Trango B-52

autolocking carabiner A carabiner with a spring-loaded gate that locks automatically when you close the gate

back-clip Clipping the rope backwards though a protection carabiner, so the rope runs through the carabiner toward the rock. This increases the chance that the rope could snap across the gate and accidentally unclip.

belay Managing the rope to protect a climber, catch him if he falls, hold him if he hangs, and lower him when it's time to come down, aided by the friction of the belay device; also refers to belay station

belay anchor An anchor, usually multipoint, that the team uses to secure a belay station

belay device Any of several devices that creates sharp bends in the rope to provide friction for belaying or rappelling

belay loop A sewn loop on the front of all good rock climbing harnesses, most commonly used for clipping the belay or rappel device to a climber, and sometimes used to connect the climber to an anchor system

bent-gate carabiner A carabiner with its gate bent inward for easy rope clipping

beta Information about the moves, protection, strategy, or other knowledge, given either before or during the ascent, that may help a climber ascend a route

big wall A tall cliff that normally requires multiple days to ascend

bight Any bend in the rope that does not cross itself; used for creating many knots, and to thread the rope into belay/ rappel devices

bolt An anchor consisting of a metal bolt set in a drilled hole that expands in the hole when tightened, creating friction which secures the bolt in place; also could be a metal bolt glued into the hole with epoxy; an accompanying hanger provides an attachment point for clipping a carabiner;

well-placed bolts $3/8$-inch or more in diameter are suitable for rock climbing anchors; smaller diameter bolts should be considered dangerous

bombproof A completely reliable anchor; also called a *bomber*

bouldering Climbing without a rope, usually close to the ground where a fall does not have bad consequences

cam Common term for spring-loaded camming device; also refers to the individual camming lobes in a camming device; also used as a verb, when a downward force is dispersed into the crack walls as an outward force, creating friction to oppose the downward pull

carabiner A high-strength aluminum snaplink used to connect parts of a climbing system

chock Term for "artificial chockstone"; a climbing anchor that wedges in a constriction for security, including hexagonal chocks and nuts

chockstone A stone wedged naturally in a crack; may or may not be solid

cleaning Removing protection anchors from a climb

clove hitch A hitch used for tying a rope into an anchor, or connecting some gear to the rope; often used by the climber to clip into the belay anchors because it is easy to adjust the tie-in length

coil A bend in rope or webbing that crosses over itself

cord Round accessory cord up to 7 mm in diameter made of high-strength materials; used for cordelettes, slinging chocks, and for making short loops

cordelette A 16- to 25-foot piece of cord, usually between 5.5 mm and 7 mm in diameter, and often tied into a loop; it performs many tasks, including building belay anchors and aiding in self-rescue

crux The hardest move or series of moves on a pitch; the hardest pitch on a multi-pitch climb

double fisherman A standard knot for joining two ropes together, or tying a piece of cord into a loop

double-length sling A sling that, when folded in half, fits nicely over the climber's shoulder

dyno A dynamic move where the climber pushes on the footholds and pulls on the handholds to gain momentum, then flies upward to catch a far-away hold

dynamic belay A technique where the belayer intentionally lets some rope slip through the belay device in a leader fall to decrease the impact force on the climber and anchors

dynamic rope A climbing rope that stretches under load to absorb the kinetic energy of a falling climber without allowing the impact force to become so great as to injure the climber or break the anchors

equalize Tying the anchors together so they share any load, ideally they share it equally

ERNEST A set of principles for constructing belay anchors: Equalized, Redundant, No Extension, Strong, and Timely

extension A potential extending of slings or cords in an anchor system caused by failure of a single point; can create a higher impact force on the remaining anchors

fall factor A measure of the severity of a fall; calculated by dividing the length of the fall by the length of rope in the system; the greater the fall factor, the greater the impact force on the anchors, climber, and belayer

figure eight knot A knot shaped like an 8; used for tying the rope into the harness, tying two ropes together, tying a loop for clipping into anchors or connecting a haul pack to the rope, et cetera

fixed protection Any permanent anchor point; usually a bolt, piton, or permanently set chock or cam

four cam unit A camming unit with four cam lobes; often stronger than a three cam unit

free climbing Climbing using only the hands, feet, and body to make progress, with the climbing protection used only to prevent a fall, and never to support body weight

free-soloing Climbing a route without a rope; a fall can be, and often is, fatal

friction hitch Any of several hitches that will lock onto the rope when loaded, yet can be slid along the rope when not loaded; most often used for self-rescue techniques

gate flutter The fast, repeated opening and closing of a carabiner gate that can occur when the rope runs through it during a fall

girth hitch A hitch used to connect a sling or loop of cord to an object by wrapping it around the object and through itself

GriGri An auto-locking belay device made by Petzl

half rope A rope designed to be used in pairs, but the individual ropes can be clipped separately into protection points to reduce rope drag

hand crack A crack the right size for setting hand jams

hanging belay A belay stance with no ledge, so the climbers must hang in their harnesses

hexagonal chock An asymmetrical, six-sided chock that wedges into three different sizes of cracks

hitch A type of knot where a rope or cord fastens around an object; without the object, the hitch would come undone

HMS carabiner A large, pear-shaped carabiner that works great with a Münter hitch

horn A spike of rock that can be used for an anchor or hold

impact force The peak load developed in a leader fall; the force is greatest on the top anchor

kilonewton (kN) A metric measurement of force; one kilonewton equals 225 pounds

lap coil A method of stacking the rope back and forth over the belayer's tie-in at hanging belays

lap link An open, steel ring with overlapping ends that are hammered together after the ring is placed around something; often used to connect rappel ropes to fixed rappel anchors; sometimes used as a lowering ring on sport routes

lead climbing Climbing first up a pitch and placing protection as you go

leader The person leading a pitch or climb

lead fall A fall taken while leading; the leader falls twice the distance to the last piece of protection

locking carabiner A carabiner with a gate that locks closed to prevent it from accidentally opening

lock off Holding the body in position with one arm while the other reaches for the next hold or high protection

lowering Descending by hanging on the rope and being lowered by the belayer; the common method of descent from a slingshot top rope or sport climb

master point The main attachment loop in a belay or rappel anchor

multidirectional anchor An anchor that can hold a load in any direction

multi-pitch route A climb that must be climbed in multiple pitches, with intermediate belays

Munter hitch A hitch that creates friction on the rope, used for belaying and rappelling

natural protection An anchor made from a natural feature such as a tree, boulder, chockstone, horn, or rock tunnel

nut Term for wedge-shaped anchors that lock into constrictions in a crack to create an anchor

nut tool A thin metal pick used to help loosen and remove stuck protection or to clean cracks

objective hazard A hazard that cannot be controlled by the climber: for example, rockfall, lightning, weather

off-width crack A crack that is too wide for fists and too small to fit the body; one of the more difficult and despised types of climbing

on-sight To lead a route first try without falling or hanging on the rope, and without any prior knowledge about the moves, strategy, or protection; the finest style in which to ascend a route

opposition Using anchors to oppose each other to create a multi-directional anchor

overhanging A section of rock that is steeper than vertical

pitch The section of a climb between belays; a pitch climbs from one belay station to the next

piton A "steel spike" that is hammered into a crack to create an anchor; an eye on the piton provides an attachment point. Pitons are fixed in place on some traditional routes that might be hard to protect with nuts and cams, and fixed pitons may or may not be reliable anchors

pocket A hole in the rock that forms a hand- or foothold, and sometimes a place to set protection

protection point A rock anchor that a leader clips the rope to for safety if a fall occurs; often called *pro*

Prusik A friction hitch used in self-rescue systems; creates the highest friction among the friction knots included in this book

pulley effect The potential doubling of the impact force on the top anchor because it must hold the force on the falling climber *and* the force on the belayer

quickdraw A short sling with a carabiner clipped to each end, used for connecting the rope to bolts and nuts, or for extending the protection on an anchor to minimize bending of the rope

rack The collection of protection anchors, slings, quickdraws, et cetera that climbers carry up a route to build the protection system

rappel A method used for descending a rope in order to return to the ground

rappel anchor Any anchor used to hold the rope when rappelling

rappel backup A friction hitch used to back up the brake hand when rappelling

rappel device A device, often used also for belaying, that creates friction on the rope so a climber can control his or her rappel

rappel ring A metal ring, preferably steel, attached to a fixed anchor; the rope is threaded through the ring (usually two or more rings attached to two or more anchors) to anchor the rope for rappelling or lowering

re-direct Changing the direction of pull on a rope by rerouting it through an anchor; often used to run the climber's rope up to a high anchor and back to the belayer, thereby decreasing the load on the belayer, and pulling the belayer up rather than down

redpoint To climb a route without falling after previous effort spent working out the moves

redundant Relying on more than a single link in the protection system; if a single point fails one or more backups exist

rest position Any body position that takes weight off the arms for a rest

rock fall Rocks falling from above as a result of either natural or human causes; an objective hazard that climbers need to be aware of and avoid

rope bag A nylon sack used to carry and protect the rope

rope drag Friction caused by the rope running over the rock and through carabiners; increases with each bend in the rope

rope tarp A fabric mat for stacking the rope on the ground; to move to another route you roll up the tarp, move it, and unroll the tarp, without having to coil the rope; extremely convenient when climbing multiple single pitch routes

runout A section on a climb with a long distance between protection points, either because the protection was not available, or because the climber chose not to set it

sandbag To mislead a climber regarding the difficulty or danger of a route; not cool because it can be dangerous

screw gate A locking carabiner that locks shut when the gate is turned a few rotations

second The climber who follows the leader up a pitch, cleaning the protection as he or she goes, with a top rope from the leader for safety

seconding The act of following and cleaning a pitch

self-rescue The act of rescuing your own team in the event of a mishap, using only the standard climbing equipment that you are carrying

sheath The woven nylon outer layer of a rope that protects the core

shoulder sling A piece of webbing sewn or tied into a loop, just long enough to comfortably fit over the climber's shoulder

simul-belay The act of belaying two climbers who follow a pitch at the same time; sometimes used by advanced climbers or guides for rapidly moving a team of three

single rope A dynamic climbing rope rated to be used by itself for protecting a lead climber or second

slab A rock face that is less than vertical

slings Webbing sewn or tied into a loop; typically shoulder length to triple shoulder length

slingshot top rope The most common system for top-roping; the rope passes from the climber, up to the anchors at the top of the route, and back down to the belayer who is stationed on the ground

sport climbing Climbing where all the protection consists of fixed bolts; usually single-pitch routes where the climber is lowered back to the ground after completing the climb

squeeze chimney A chimney just wide enough to barely admit the climber's body

stacking the rope Uncoiling the rope into a loose pile with the top and bottom ends exposed; the leader ties into the top end; minimizes tangles; also called flaking the rope

static elongation The amount a rope will stretch when holding a body-weight load

static rope A climbing rope that stretches little so it works great for hauling, top roping, or ascending a fixed line, but it is not suitable for lead climbing

stemming Using footholds in opposition to get weight off the hands, and to increase the security of marginal footholds; often used in inside corners

stick-clip To clip the rope to the first bolt on a route by attaching a carabiner or quickdraw to a long stick; prevents a ground fall if the climber falls in the beginning of the route

stopper knot A knot tied in the end of a rope to keep a climber from rappelling or being lowered off the end of the rope

subjective hazard A hazard that can be usually controlled by good judgment or conservatism on the part of the climber

tail The rope end that sticks out after tying a knot

thread Any naturally occurring tunnel in the rock that a sling may be passed through to create an anchor

three cam unit A camming unit with three cams; often weaker than a four cam unit, but fits into shallow cracks

triple-length sling A sling that, when folded into thirds, fits nicely over a climber's shoulder

top-rope anchor The belay anchor for a top-rope

top-rope fall A fall while climbing on a top-rope; usually very short unless there is slack in the system

topo A map of a route using symbols to show the rock features, belays, and fixed protection

traditional (trad) climbing Climbing a route where the leader sets protection points along the way, to be removed later by the second; as opposed to sport climbing

transition The steps required to change from one climbing system to another, for example, from climbing to rappelling

traverse A section on a climb or boulder problem that moves sideways rather than up

tri-axial loading A situation where a carabiner is pulled in three directions, weakening the carabiner

Tri-cam An anchor that can be wedged into a constriction in a crack, or cammed into a parallel crack; extremely versatile, but not always stable

twin ropes Thin ropes that must be used in pairs, with both ropes clipped into all protection points; provides two ropes for rappelling

UIAA The Union Internationale des Associations d'Alpinism; the international association of national climbing clubs that sets standards for and tests climbing safety equipment

walking The tendency for camming units to move in the crack when wriggled by the climbing rope; can compromise the placement; often negated by clipping the rope in with a long extension

water knot The standard knot for tying webbing into a loop; a retraced overhand knot

webbing Nylon fibers woven flat like a strap; used for making slings

wedge To lock a chock or nut into place in a constricting section of a crack

wire-gate carabiner A carabiner with a gate made of wire instead of solid aluminum stock; decreases weight and minimizes the chance of having the gate vibrate open in a fall, which can cause the carabiner to break

Resources

CLIMBING ORGANIZATIONS

Access Fund, P.O. Box 17010, Boulder, CO
80308; (303) 545-6772; *www.accessfund.org*

American Alpine Club, 710 Tenth Street,
Golden, CO 80401; (303) 384-0110;
www.americanalpineclub.org

American Mountain Guides Association,
P.O. Box 1739, Boulder, CO 80302;
(303) 271-0984; *www.amga.com*

Leave No Trace, P.O. Box 997, Boulder, CO
80306; (303) 442-8222; *www.lnt.org*

The Mountaineers Club, 300 Third Ave.
West, Seattle, WA 98119; (206) 284-6310;
www.mountaineers.org

CLIMBING WEBSITES

www.alpinist.com
www.climbing.com
www.climbing-gyms.com
www.cubaclimbing.com
www.frontrangebouldering.com
www.johngill.net
www.jwharper.com
www.mountainproject.com
www.naclassics.com
www.neclimbs.com
www.neice.com
www.newenglandbouldering.com
www.planetmountain.com
www.redriverclimbing.com
www.rockandice.com
www.rockclimbing.com
www.southeastclimbing.com
www.supertopo.com
www.texasclimbers.com

The author's website highlights his climbing, guiding, writing, and photography, as well as updates on information contained in this book: *www.craigluebben.com*

Please send comments and criticisms of this book to the author at: *cluebben@aol.com*

Index

About the Author

Craig Luebben started guiding and instructing rock and ice climbing in 1981. He is an American Mountain Guides Association certified rock guide and currently teaches rock guide courses for AMGA. He designed Big Bro expandable tube chocks as a mechanical engineering student at Colorado State University; while testing the Big Bro chocks he became a specialist in off-width cracks. For over twenty years he has studied and tested climbing anchor systems.

He serves as safety director and guide for Lynn Hill Climbing Camps, and writes as senior contributing editor for *Climbing* magazine. He has written *Knots for Climbers*, *Advanced Rock Climbing* (with John Long), *How to Ice Climb*, *How to Rappel*, *Betty and the Silver Spider: An Introduction to Gym Climbing*, and *Rock Climbing: Mastering Basic Skills*.

Craig has opened new rock and ice routes across the United States, and in Canada, Mexico, Cuba, France, Italy, Greece, China, and Madagascar. He has climbed numerous wall routes in Yosemite Valley, Zion Canyon, and Black Canyon of the Gunnison, and cragged at hundreds of other areas. He lives in Golden, Colorado with his wife Silvia and daughter Giulia.

THE MOUNTAINEERS, founded in 1906, is a nonprofit outdoor activity and conservation club, whose mission is "to explore, study, preserve, and enjoy the natural beauty of the outdoors. . . . " Based in Seattle, Washington, the club is now the third-largest such organization in the United States, with seven branches throughout Washington State.

The Mountaineers sponsors both classes and year-round outdoor activities in the Pacific Northwest, which include hiking, mountain climbing, ski-touring, snowshoeing, bicycling, camping, kayaking, nature study, sailing, and adventure travel. The club's conservation division supports environmental causes through educational activities, sponsoring legislation, and presenting informational programs.

All club activities are led by skilled, experienced instructors, who are dedicated to promoting safe and responsible enjoyment and preservation of the outdoors.

If you would like to participate in these organized outdoor activities or the club's programs, consider a membership in The Mountaineers. For information and an application, write or call The Mountaineers, Club Headquarters, 300 Third Avenue West, Seattle, WA 98119; 206-284-6310. You can also visit the club's website at www.mountaineers.org or contact The Mountaineers via email at clubmail@mountaineers.org.

The Mountaineers Books, an active, nonprofit publishing program of the club, produces guidebooks, instructional texts, historical works, natural history guides, and works on environmental conservation. All books produced by The Mountaineers Books fulfill the club's mission.

Send or call for our catalog of more than 500 outdoor titles:

 The Mountaineers Books
1001 SW Klickitat Way, Suite 201
Seattle, WA 98134
800-553-4453

mbooks@mountaineersbooks.org
www.mountaineersbooks.org

 The Mountaineers Books is proud to be a corporate sponsor of The Leave No Trace Center for Outdoor Ethics, whose mission is to promote and inspire responsible outdoor recreation through education, research, and partnerships. The Leave No Trace program is focused specifically on human-powered (nonmotorized) recreation.
Leave No Trace strives to educate visitors about the nature of their recreational impacts, as well as offer techniques to prevent and minimize such impacts. Leave No Trace is best understood as an educational and ethical program, not as a set of rules and regulations.
For more information, visit *www.LNT.org*, or call 800-332-4100.

MORE CLIMBING TITLES FROM THE TOP ATHLETES AND ORGANIZATIONS IN THE SPORT

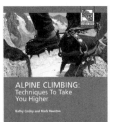

Mountaineering: The Freedom of the Hills, 7th Ed.
The Mountaineers Club
The all-time best selling standard reference for the sport of climbing.

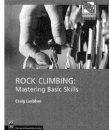

Rock Climbing: Mastering Basic Skills
Craig Luebben
For beginner to intermediate climbers.

Alpine Climbing: Techniques to Take You Higher
Kathy Cosley and Mark Houston
Master the process of situational decision-making in the mountains.

Big Wall Climbing: Elite Technique
Jared Ogden
Skills and strategies unique to big walls.

Ice & Mixed Climbing: Modern Technique
Will Gadd
Expand your climbing chops with instructions from the best.

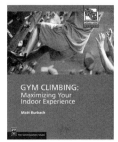

Gym Climbing: Maximizing Your Indoor Experience
Matt Burbach
Urban climbing for new climbers, climbers staying in shape, and climbers who find all the challenge they desire indoors.

Climbing: Training for Peak Performance
Clyde Soles
Build the muscles you need for this ultimate of muscle-powered sports.

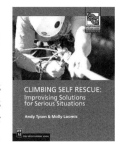

Climbing Self-Rescue: Improvising Solutions for Serious Situations
Andy Tyson & Molly Loomis
How to get yourself and others out of a jam without calling 911.

The Mountaineers Books has more than 500 outdoor recreation titles in print.
Receive a free catalog at
www.mountaineersbooks.org.